# BY CHANCE

## RICK SHORTLE

authorHOUSE®

*AuthorHouse™ UK*
*1663 Liberty Drive*
*Bloomington, IN 47403  USA*
*www.authorhouse.co.uk*
*Phone: UK TFN: 0800 0148641 (Toll Free inside the UK)*
*        UK Local: (02) 0369 56322 (+44 20 3695 6322 from outside the UK)*

*Published by AuthorHouse  01/19/2023*

*ISBN: 979-8-8230-8019-4 (sc)*
*ISBN: 979-8-8230-8020-0 (hc)*
*ISBN: 979-8-8230-8018-7 (e)*

*Thanks to my grandson Cameron Patrick Lee for the fantastic front and rear cover design and thanks to Neil Connor for helping me proof this book and at the same time keeping it to my style of writing as many commented about my first book, Full Circle, an Autobiography, that it was like talking to Rick in his front room.*

# CONTENTS

# INTRODUCTION BY BRIAN VARNEY

I have known Rick for 40 years, and throughout this time, his loves have always been first family, married over 50 years, and second motor racing.

I first saw an article in our local newspaper referring to this talented plasterer seeking sponsorship to race the Getem ff1600 in the Champion of Brands.

At the time, I was much younger, more prosperous, and enjoyed F1, the Nigel Mansel era, so I got in touch. We organised the RS Consortium of individuals and small businesses and raised the necessary sponsorship and racing.

Getem was a homemade car, and up against top race car manufacturers. Van Dieman (still a leading Formula Ford) and Reynard (who were challenging them for supremacy and went on to build Formula Three race cars). Both manufacturers ran Works teams with massive budgets.

After achieving some success, more success than we could have imagined. We changed cars to the Reynard 84, in my opinion, the best and on par with the Van Dieman; Rick continued his successes supported by another team, "Rob Cresswell Racing Services."

My most fantastic memory is of him in a photo when he was in the front row, competing against the best drivers in Formula Ford 1600 from around the world. In a support race to the 1985 European F1 Grand Prix, with Nigel Mansel in the foreground. Unfortunately, the gearbox got stuck in second gear, causing Rick to retire.

The only time he did not achieve the success he deserved, was in 1985. When noting the disproportionate success of the car and funds he had, the top manufacturer Reynard offered to give him their latest car and works support for a much-reduced price. Unfortunately, it proved a significant failure and set us back a year. Undeterred, we rented a replacement car and carried on with further success in Formula Ford 1600 and 2000, Sports 2000 and Honda CRX.

All this was achieved due to Rick's boundless energy and enthusiasm, taking challenges head-on. He recovered from adversity several times in his personal and racing life in Speedway and Motor Racing. He thrived to succeed in everything he did at will; hopefully, you have read *Full Circle,* the first volume of his Autobiography. If not, I recommend that you purchase it straight away!

Even now, 40 years later, he is still involved in helping to raise sponsorship and mentor other drivers, including an up-and-coming young gun, Matt Luff, who has contested the Milltek Honda Civic Cup over the last couple of years.

Long may it continue, Rick, my good friend and a inspiration to many. Good luck with this second volume of your Autobiography; you deserve it.

Brian Varney
Ashford
Kent

# INTRODUCTION BY RUSSELL HOUCHIN

12 years ago, Rick wrote his life story for the grandchildren possibly. Now he's back with the sequel to that successful Autobiography *Full Circle* in which he encapsulates his full racing career. It's a fascinating insight into motor racing in a very different era with vivid memories, archive material and photos from his career. A race drivers read, pure and simple, for those who love the sport and have been involved in its many dimensions: the ups and downs, paddock camaraderie, racing incidents of course, the three on the race podiums and the thousands of other drivers making up the grid, without whom the sport cannot thrive and endure. Every Race driver can relate to the author's tales, and warm to a guy who loved the thrill and spills of the racetracks in the UK and Europe.

Russell Houchin
Sponsor for over 40 years
Milton Keynes.

# BY CHANCE

My first book, *Full Circle An Autobiography,* proved to be more successful than I could have imagined. Many that have read it say it's like chatting with Rick in his front room, so I'm not going to change how I write my books because it works for me, and you, the reader.

My next book, *By Chance,* will tell the story of my racing years.. I was fortunate enough to have raced in ff1600 in what were my best years ever—the 1980s. Grids often oversubscribed some meetings, I.E., the Silverstone Esso and John Player Champion of Brands would run a couple of heats to make the final. The list of outstanding drivers in that decade was endless, Senna, Johnny Herbert, Roland Ratzenberger, Welsh Wizard Karl Jones, Eddie Irvine, Peter Rogers, Damon Hill, Rick Morris, John Village, Dave Coyne, John Pratt-Perry McCarthy, and Chris Hall. The Rain Master, to name but a few.

The title of my book, *By Chance,* is what happened. It allowed me by chance to take advantage of the many opportunities that seemed to come my way, and it was up to me to make sure I grabbed these opportunities with both hands.

Because I was dedicated, committed and wanted to win, I became relatively successful in contested formulas. Yes, I won many races, and I'm sure quite a few of you may even have raced against me during the 1980s - 90s.

Like most of us, we never reached the dizzy heights of Formula One. It doesn't mean there isn't a story to tell because there is, so read on as this book will hopefully bring back memories to many of you, and maybe those who fancied racing might spur you on.

This time, my book *By Chance* is for all you motor racing fans; to explain how I got into and eventually earned a living out of the Motor Sports Industry. The great friends I made, and the personalities, I gave tuition.

For many reasons, I consider the following my golden years; therefore, a bulk share of this book is about Formula Ford's 1600 days. I.E. my success, my sponsors and the people I was involved with, the teams I raced for, the drivers I raced against and all sorts of things we all did to get onto the grid back in the eighties and 90s. Not forgetting, that for me, a few broken bones were had along the way!

Let my book ***By Chance*** begin!

# CHAPTER 1

## GRASS TRACK

Getting into motor racing was purely by chance. On the way to work one day, all are chatting while swaying to and fro in the back of the Van; there were no seats in those days, just a scaffold board straddling the wheel arches. I mentioned to Derek Gurr, one of the plasterers, that I had been chatting with a guy about Grasstrack racing; we had a great chat he told me all about it. I knew that Derek followed Grasstrack racing; he said they were off to a weekend meeting. I was going to a grass track meeting, he replied. Following grass track racing was his thing. Finding it somewhat intriguing, I half-heartedly suggested to Derek that maybe we should buy a bike between us and see how we get on.

Grass track racing back in the 70s and 80s pulled in large crowds. It was enjoyable for the whole family to watch and get involved. Organising Clubs would approach farmers to hire a good-sized flattish field for the weekend. They would set an oval track up to 650 meters, similar to a speedway track, but grass and usually grass tracks are bumpy. Being me, one to never let the grass grow under my feet, excuse the pun, I decided to go along to see what grass track racing was all about. We lived in Ashford, Kent, only a few miles from Romney Marsh, where grass track race meetings were on the calendar several times a year. The fields are of excellent quality, probably because Romney Marsh is famous for the Sheep that graze everywhere, keeping the grass short, ideal for grass tracks. The next meeting at Romney Marsh was, by chance, just a couple of weeks away. I certainly didn't have any idea of what was in store. A couple of

Sundays later, I was on my way to watch my first-ever grass track meeting. From the moment I entered the field, I was buzzing. There was something about the feel of it, the noise of the bikes racing, the carnival atmosphere. But most of all, it was the Castrol R oil the competitors put into the bike engines. The smell was amazing. Well, Mr Gur, you've been and started something now.

I spent most of the day watching these nutters' leg trailing, tearing around a 650-meter oval. The show's stars were the sidecar racers; they must have left their brains in their toolboxes.

Before the end of the day, I talked with several riders, and I encouraged Derek to buy something in the 250cc class before joining the fast Boys in the 500cc class. So, we were; owners of a 250CC grass bike and didn't even know how to look after it. Let alone race it. We had to find out how to go racing. We soon learned it wasn't a case of chucking a grass bike in the back of a van and going racing. We needed to join a club, apply for race licenses, and get some practice in sharpish. I managed to locate a field from a local farmer, who loved a drink, so we gave him a bottle of his favourite tipple, whiskey, every time we practised on his field. Derek, a bit of a woose after falling off a couple of times, decided to throw the towel in, which caused a problem because he owned 50% of the Bike. If I wanted to continue, I had to give him his half back in cash.

I was still up for it; I decided to sell the 250cc as a deposit against a brand new 500cc Palmer Jap engined Bike. It was going to be several weeks before it would be ready. The bike builder came from Maidstone, Kent, not too far away. I often visited his Workshop to see how things were getting on; it was exciting to see the bike coming together.

I collected my brand new Palmer grass bike two months before the race season, allowing me to practice.

My first-ever grass track race was looming rapidly, and I must admit to being somewhat apprehensive. Up to now, I have only owned a road bike for a few months. Before it got stolen by a known troublemaker, a Lad named Ginger Briley from Cranbrook Kent. Ginger had a big accident, smashing my Bike up and injuring himself badly. Therefore my experience of riding a motorcycle was somewhat limited. For me, grass track racing was only to last a season, As, by chance, I was about to be encouraged to swap grass track to the fast and furious world as a Speedway Rider. A shame because I had already achieved a 3$^{rd}$, 2$^{nd}$, and 1$^{st}$.

# CHAPTER 2

―――■◆■―――

# SPEEDWAY

By chance, I met Brian and Celia Elma, owners of the A.B.C. Stores Hythe Road Ashford Kent, my regular food and drink stop to take to the grass track meetings. One morning Brian asked how my grass track racing was doing. Brian and Celia were mad about speedway racing. At the time, I'd never heard of it. I soon learned about it from Brian. After seeing Brian and Celia regularly, I.E., my regular food and drink stop. He approached me to see if I would be interested in racing Speedway and if I said yes, he would sponsor me. Buy the Bike and take me around the country to the race meetings. He suggested we go to our closest track to watch Speedway. The Canterbury Crusaders. Managed by Johnny Hoskins, who bought Speedway in England in the 1950s. And by the 70s, it was a major attraction throughout the British Isles.

Speedway meetings were mainly in the evening, which gave it far more appeal as dusk drew near. The whole track was floodlit, creating a great atmosphere. Little did Brian know, I loved the idea of becoming a Speedway Rider.

When we returned to Brian's Flat above the shop, we had a long chat into the early hours. As Brian was the expert, I listened to his every word; the more he talked, the more I wanted it. The first thing to do was buy a speedway bike. Watching Speedway in action was incredible. I couldn't believe how these riders could put these bikes around a reasonably small Oval at such a great speed, without brakes, and getting so close to each other is unbelievable. Bikes in fashion were the Jawa 500cc set in a Godden frame. It ran a total loss oil system in the bike frame, which is not much bigger than a pushbike. The oil went into the frame; the Castrol R would circulate through the engine, then drip out onto the track. Giving out that fabulous smell I first experienced at the grass track meeting. These machines have no brakes, 0 to 60 in 2.8 seconds. I still feel racing and sliding a speedway bike is fantastic, exciting, dangerous, and bloody good fun. Brian accepted I was green with anything to do with Speedway Racing.

We needed to go and visit all the circuits up and down the country to practice, practice, practice, which we did. When Brian thought I got to a standard good enough, he would book me into a Speedway training school run by the top drivers of the time. Dave Jessop, John Davis World Champion Peter Collins, would give you advice, and if you were any good, one of the tracks might sign you up. We chose Reading Races. It was a Division One team. First, a schoolroom chat, and then we went out on our bikes. I found it an unbelievable experience to be racing under the supervision of all the top riders.

I was one of 10 riders hoping to be signed by Reading Racers after the three-day course, and only three riders would be that lucky. For me, the first day went well. Winning all my heats, the 2nd day to midday mirrored the first day. After lunch, it was more of the same. In my second heat after lunch, I caught the fence with my handlebars, snapping my collarbone, apparently a common thing in Speedway. I still have the battle scar to this very day. I.E.! An irritating overlapping collar bone.

I was so upset and annoyed as I wanted to ride for Reading Racers. Sponsor Brian Elmer took me to Reading General Hospital. They fitted a collar and cuff and sent us on our way. I phoned my wife Anne and said all was good as I didn't want to worry her. Reading Racers said they would like me to attend the presentation the following day. However, it was pretty painful travelling. Brian felt we should show our faces as it would be good P.R.

We made the presentation in plenty of time, which allowed us to mingle and chat with the other nine riders. I must admit to feeling pissed off and knowing I didn't have a chance of getting one of those three places to become a Reading Racers Rider.

Dave Jessup! Rider for England and Captain of Reading Racers did the presentations. Dave did a bit of chit-chat on how the three-day course went. Then we waited to hear which three riders would receive a contract to Race for Division One Team Reading Racers.

Dave started with the usual stuff, 3$^{rd}$, 2$^{nd}$ and 1$^{st}$. He remarked in third place. A driver showed a lot of promise; sadly, he argued with the fence on the 2$^{nd}$ day, and if he had completed the three days, Rick Shortle would have been a contender for first place. I couldn't believe what I was hearing.

So with great pride and a tear in my eye, I stepped up to receive my cup and Contract to Race for Reading Racers, Mega.

Brian was delighted and quite emotional; our long journey home went in a flash because of nonstop excitement and chattering. Brian suggested we get the latest Speedway Bike, a Godden Weslake. The next day, we called Don Godden to order a bike. We chose a chrome bike with a chequered flag effect saddle. It's funny how things would change as my story moves forward. Would you believe I've never been to Brands Hatch or couldn't have dreamt what was on the cards for me? But for the moment, it's Bikes and nothing but Bikes.

During my transition from Grasstrack to Speedway, I discovered that an outstanding Speedway Rider named Reg Luckhurst was currently racing for division One Team Wimbledon Dons. Reg lived in the next village to me; he had a good business repairing grass and speedway bikes, used by many riders that required spares or repairs. During my time as a Speedway rider, I got to know Reg very well, and he gave me loads of advice. I even did a couple of plastering jobs for him (my trade at the time). I also met some of the Stars of that era. IE Dave Jessup- Peter Collins- John Davis-Malcolm Simmonds-Ollie Nigren-Michael Lee E.T.C. Reg makes the Speedway Racks which bolt onto the back of the car, a great invention by Reg Luckhurst, used by every speedway Rider in the Country. An excellent way for riders to carry their Bike to the meetings.

In the background, A.B.C. STORE's owners and sponsors were beavering away, booking me into speedway tracks Nationwide. As we aimed to get as competitive as possible before the next season began, for now, I had to make do with the Jawa until my Godden Weslake was ready. Brian had booked me to race at Pool-Eastbourne-Iwade-Hackney-Mildenhall, next door to the American Air Base.-Reading-Wimbledon-Kings Lynn-Ipswich.

Our pre-season campaign was brilliant. Every track put together a meeting so the riders could treat it like the real thing. Many riders attending all ready raced for teams, giving a good idea of what to expect when the season starts.

My first Race for Reading Racers was a (Home Meeting), a second-half race to Race against top division One riders: a massive moment, my first-ever meeting racing against some of the best riders in the world. The line-up in my Race is, in gate one, my good self' Gate two, Kings Lynn World Champion Peter Collins - Gate three Reading Racers John Davis - Gate four Kings Lynn Bernie Lee.

More luck than judgment. I out-gated the other three riders and took the lead into the first corner. I felt the other three riders breathing down my neck; I hung in there but went back to last. (to be expected), I was thrilled with my first-ever Race for Reading Racers. I had a couple of races that evening and got a third in the other Races and my first payslip as a speedway rider.

Things were certainly looking good. Because of my early promise, the team manager got in touch and advised that I would be farmed out to my local track Canterbury Crusaders. I was thrilled things were moving forward so quickly. The new season was only a few weeks away, as usual. My manager/ Sponsor, Brian, booked me in for some practice.

The first outing was at one of my favourite tracks, the Hackney Hawks. London.

Progress was undoubtedly going well; all I could think about was Speedway; it seemed to be taking over my life. Whilst this is all going on,

I'm busy with my plastering business which, thank the Lord, was going great guns.

So this is my final practice before I race for Canterbury Crusaders as one of their Riders. I'm ecstatic and cannot wait to walk out under a floodlit arena to wave to the fans.

Before all that, there is business to do at Hackney. I'm looking forward to rolling up with my beautiful Godden Weslake, racing around my favourite track and strutting about in the pits, but only if I'm doing well.

The day has arrived. We made it through Hackney via the Blackwall Tunnel; it was a good run. We even parked before the office was open. I hate hanging around and need to be doing something; otherwise, I tend to overthink; I used to think Brian was far more nervous than I.

At last, the office opened, so we could sign on and take our Bikes to the pit area. Get sorted and wait for the track to open. In the meantime, I nipped to the changing rooms to get into my leathers, boots, etc. and not forget the steel shoe required on your left shoe to help your boot slide quickly as you use it with cornering.

Whilst I was changing into my leathers. A chap wearing a business suit and carrying a briefcase by chance appeared. He introduced himself as a representative for Canadian Life. He opened his briefcase. He explained that Canadian Life would insure us for our racing activities, including paying the mortgage any H.P. you may have, plus a weekly amount.

He went on to explain if I signed on the dotted line now. I would be fully covered immediately. I thought, bugger it, I will sign, so I did. More of this later. I couldn't wait for him to leave; I only wanted to get on my Brand new Godden Westlake Bike delivered the day before. It certainly created a lot of interest as it sat on the bike stand in the Pits, even Hackney Hawks Manager. Len Silver (great name) stopped to look and chat. Brian gets chuffed with things like that; I was donning my new leathers in Norfolk colours, I.E., Yellow and Green, not my first choice. Still, Brian supports the Canaries, so Yellow and Green it is.

We looked the part, and it will soon be up to me to do the business. It's getting very near playtime; all the bikes are sitting on their stands, rear-wheel clear of the ground, so you can start the engine by simply spinning the wheel. It is incredible to see all the bike wheels turning whilst the riders warm their bikes up. The number of bikes greatly enhances the fantastic smell of Castrol R.

Looking down the line of bikes, I notice the rider's helmets are going on, and the bikes are dropping off the stands, so here we go. You best get in line so you're ready to join the track. Races run like formal meetings.

My first Race will be to get a feel of this new Goodden Westlake! I started from gate four, and we were allowed a couple of laps of practice, giving me an idea of what to expect. First, it was quick and easy to lift the front wheel; apart from that, it was a dream to ride. I was at home with my new steed straight away. I finished third without too much bother; roll on to Race two.

I couldn't wait to get out again. I was fortunate enough to get another four races, of which I won two and came second in the other two; needless to say, we were buzzing. The clock was ticking; not much time left for another race. Brian and I agreed that if we were quick, we might make one more Race. I'm elated just managed to get a race, and this will be my last Race until I walk out for the first time with the Reading Racer Team at our home track! To wave to the fans before the meeting I can't wait. But first, we have this Race which I want to win. I'm in gate two, trying to find a track to give grip. It should help make a good start, a bit of to & fro with your Bike until the gate Marshall tells you to hold station. Next, you position yourself on your Bike to balance your weight; next, the most crucial bit of being first out of the gate. You look to the right and concentrate on the tapes going into the sliding tower. You are looking for a spark; see it first and coordinate it; getting out of your gate means getting into the first corner.

In my short time as a racer, I got into the habit of saying just before the tapes went up / lights turned to green. (that corners mine)—something I did through all my future races, including car racing.

Through your helmet, you can hear the scream of the Westlake engines, all holding on to the chosen revs for an excellent start, tapes fly up, we all leave the start together, into the first corner, all 4 of us laying on each other, as we all exit turn two I lose a place putting me in third place, into turn three I manage to get alongside the second-placed rider and exit turn four behind the leading rider, with three laps to go I had time to nick first place, I held station for the next lap, the leading rider seems to take turn three wide around the outside, I decided to take a tight line hoping I can find the grip to allow me to get under him, my plan seems to be working I'm now on the inside of turn three and slowly getting the edge on the other driver, I now have to try and cut across to stop him from accelerating away, this is where it all goes wrong, I gain grip wind on the throttle, the front wheel lifts I can't get it down, the fence on the outside of the track that separates the track from the Dog track is getting ever nearer, then all of a sudden my bike slams into the fence with my right leg caught between the fence and the Westlake engine, everything from now on seems to be in slow motion, I was ejected from my Bike, thrown into the air and end up landing in the Dog track. I remember it as if it was yesterday; everything went silent, as if nobody was around. I felt no pain, and then from nowhere, St. Johns Ambulance arrived; they started to attend to me. I began to feel pain as they were strapping my legs together. I remember telling them there was a knot in the cord and hearing the first aid chap saying to the other, that's not a knot; that's the bone from his leg sticking through his leg.

It seemed an eternity before I was in the Ambulance on my way to Hackney Hospital.

# CHAPTER 3

## MY TIME AT HACKNEY HOSPITALL

I knew it wasn't good, and I was to find out just how serious it was a couple of days later. I was on gas and air to help relieve the pain, and soon into the ambulance and on my way to Hackney Hospital. I remember getting to the hospital, but after that, I seemed to have lost at least a day, which was a godsend. I remember waking up with a plaster cast from the tip of my toe to my groin, and I noticed a pin was protruding from either side of my heel. The Doctor explained that I had lost an inch of bone from my leg; it wasn't a clean break when I asked. It's called a complicated fracture when the bone is shattered into small pieces and could damage the veins, arteries or nerves and lining of the bone. They had to stretch my leg in the hope it would produce more bone and be ok. The surgeon also fixed a see-through plastic spy hole between the knee and ankle so they could check for any gangrene. They had already informed Anne that the shale that got into my leg could cause it to go sceptic, and there was a worry I may lose my leg. Anne kept this very quiet; bless her. Hackney Hospital was a training hospital with very high numbers of staff, which was great. The Wards back then were so long that it was a job to see the other end. Goodness knows how many beds were in each Ward. I am now dawning that this will be a long road to recovery. I wasn't aware of how long the recovery time would be, but I felt it would take a while.

My first thoughts were Anne and my two girls, Tina and Julia. How they were feeling and hoping they were ok, next to my plastering business, albeit small but doing ok. And thankfully, I had some good friends that jumped in to help. Anne was excellent; she kept it together by paying the men and ensuring our girls weren't upset. I had a good one there.

Manager and Sponsors Brian and Celia Elma were superb; he drove from Ashford in Kent to Hackney Hospital every day to visit me. Anne came when she could, and to help out, Celia would look after Tina and Julia. I was fortunate to get so much help from so many people.

In those days, the Man from the Pru, Tony Sugden, would give us a monthly visit giving that personal touch. He became a friend. So much so that when I got out of Hospital, Tony would take me around to all my plastering jobs, which was never easy having a plaster cast. He was a great help. Another chap I would like to thank is Fred Gore; he was a plasterer that worked for me until he was well into his seventies. As mentioned, I was fortunate to have good people around me. So I made a mental decision because I received this injury doing something I loved to get on with it and not feel sorry for myself. I was hospitalised for several weeks and kept pushing to go home.

Like most of us in the Hospital, we all think we are ready to head home. The journey home in Brian's car was a nightmare. With my leg plaster from the tip of my toe to my groin, I had to sit in the back with my leg wedged between the front seats, and the writing was on the wall before I got home; I would have been better off staying in Hospital. I shouldn't have pushed the Doctor to allow me to go home; he did give me strict orders on what I could and not do.

I was in plaster for over two years, which is a bloody long time in anyone's books. I had to go back for regular check-ups, which meant removing the plaster to see how it was healing; After 18 months, it wasn't healing. I was admitted back to Hackney Hospital for a bone graft. They took a bone from my hip and placed it on my leg; thankfully, it mended after another six months. At last, I was allowed to have the plaster off and let the physio begin.

# CHAPTER 4

## RECOVERY AND DECISION TIME

It was incredible getting out of this plaster; it looked horrendous, covered in dead skin and no muscle. Physio will be hard work. Brian dropped me off at home; so lovely it was to be home without plaster.

I negotiated past our car on the drive; I felt like driving it!

As soon as I got indoors, I went for the car keys, and they were not on their hook. I then remembered I said something to Anne about driving it. She had gone and hid them; I hunted high and low, as quietly as possible, dragging this lump for a leg around; I eventually found them. Crutches at the ready, I make my way out of the front door to the car. I had to find a way of getting in the car, which proved challenging to say the least, as I couldn't bend my leg. I walked using my crutches in the front garden and tried to turn my leg enough to slide into my car. Builders were working on a scaffold opposite, watching me walking up and on crutches. They knew about my accident as I often chatted with them. They were keen to see my next move as the car was running. I tried to negotiate my way into the vehicle's driver's seat; it took a while. It's a good job the cars an Automatic. "Houston", we have a problem; you only require a right leg to drive an Auto, Ahh, that's the bloody leg I broke, and at the moment, it's next to useless. Mmm, did I give up? not on your nelly.

I figured out my left leg could do the braking; I couldn't use the left leg for the throttle as the right leg was in the way; we were 50% of the way there; I could stop but couldn't go. I have a light bulb moment; I use one of the crutches; P.S. Builders is still watching. Moment of truth could I drive; the answer was yes, very slowly. I even got overtaken by a reliant Robin. The best bit about my first drive for over two and half years was when I returned, parked up in our drive, scrabbled out of the car, grabbed the crutches, looked across to the Builders, and gave them a bow; they gave me a round of applause. Job done. I'm now looking forward to a significant bollocking from Anne.

I was keen to get my leg moving as quickly as possible; this meant a lot of bending; at first, it wouldn't budge, slowing, and began to show signs of movement. Riding a pushbike was one of the best ways to do it. Start, so moving pedals is easy, I.E. hardly and bending them gently each day or so lower the saddle, so you have to turn a bit more each time. That helped. I was bending my knee in no time. Believe it or not, I was still thinking about Speedway, and so was Brian. I have been in plaster for over two years. Doing it again, thinking about it now, was absolute lunacy. A few weeks after getting out of this plaster cast, I hired a Speedway Bike. Brian took me to Kings Lynn to see how I would fair. I have to admit my heart wasn't in it. Still, I felt obligated because Brian had been such a diamond throughout my recovery. We got unloaded. I got into my leathers, Started the Bike up, then went out onto the track and did a few steady laps. I felt much better than I thought I would. So I went again and tried to get into the groove, but I knew I wouldn't be the same as before.

I pitted and got off the bike; this was the tricky bit; Brian looked happy with my progress

I had to tell Brian that I'd decided not to continue riding Speedway. He was devastated; unlike the journey home from Reading after I signed for Reading Racers, this was a very awkward journey indeed He did try to tempt me back, but I didn't want to hurt myself again. I have a wife and two daughters. I still had a lot of physio to do as I wasn't near Full recovery, and I needed to concentrate on that.

It will take a while to get fit enough to work. Do you remember I mentioned Canadian Life in the Speedway Chapter? Well, they did come good. The chap that got me to sign on the dotted line over two years ago was true to his word. At the time, I had a Mortgage, a Higher Purchase of a car, and no earnings. Canadian Life paid my mortgage-higher purchase and non-earnings and continued until I returned to work. (What a result?)

With so much time on my hands, I was getting bored. The plastering business was doing ok; I did the pricing. It ran itself apart from plasterers wanting material and wages. It wasn't good money like it is now. I didn't earn much from it, but I had that income from Canadian Life, so everything was good. It took me two and a half years to get fit enough to lead an everyday life. Plastering work dropped off, so I had to stand most of my plasterers off; lucky for me, they were self-employed. I had to return to the tools to earn a living; I was looking forward to being a spread again.

Life seemed to be returning to normal, although memories of those Grass Track and Speedway days were very much at the forefront of my mind. In particular, my spell as a Speedway rider, signing for Reading Racers, was fantastic but sadly short-lived, which I had to accept. I would never race Speedway again. A near neighbour of mine had a couple of Boys that did junior grass track racing. Their Dad, Mr Strover, asked me if I would consider coming to the meetings to help and advise with their technique etc. I jumped at the chance; it was just what I needed to get involved this time off the Bike. I got a buzz seeing the two Boys improve. Just the Tonic I needed.

So Life was good, no dramas. I was back to full fitness, albeit with an inch shorter right leg than the other. Oh well, something else to tell the Grandkids in a few years.

# CHAPTER 5

## BRANDS HATCH, HERE I COME

One day by chance, whilst waiting to see the Doctor, I picked up a magazine. I'm not a big reader, especially of magazines, so I just thumbed through it; I noticed an article on Brands Hatch. It was about a discount if you fancied driving a race car around Brands Hatch. It was called Brands Hatch Racing, run by the late great Brian Jones (Known as The Voice of Brands). So I booked it up only because I was kicking my heels and needed something to do. I knew this would be the start of becoming a race driver.

I might point out that I miss riding Speedway, and it would take a lot to get me interested in racing something on four wheels. I watched the Big Time programme a few days before my first visit to Brands Hatch. A race driver named Tim Lee Davey Won received backing for his racing in ff1600.

To my surprise, Tim was one of the instructors. On my first visit to Brands, little did I know! Tim would be our Teammate with Andy Ackerly a few years later. He competed in the "HONDA CRX CHALLENGE" is run by Peter Brigg's Team "Edenbridge Honda". My journey to Brands for this drive around Brands in a Racecar wasn't exciting, probably because I was pretty nervous. It seemed to take forever to get there; no Motorways to speak of in those days.

I finally arrived at Brands Hatch and got lost; it was nothing like a grass or speedway track. It was daunting; I followed the other cars hoping they were going too.

The main office next door to the "Kentagon" is the circuit restaurant and licenced bar, ideally situated for Circuit owner John Webb. He liked a tipple or two, and his office was only a few strides away.

I parked up and then strolled over to join the sign-on queue. Some of the drivers even had race suits on. I felt a bit awkward and decided to remark to the chap next to me who was also without a race suit dam, and I forgot my race suit, which broke the ice.

I knew nothing about motor racing or cars, teams, and drivers. My first bit of information was that the lady who signed us on was non-other than Desire Wilson, ex F1 Driver from South Africa. I was well impressed and even more nervous.

Once signed on, we made our way to the Control Tower and reported to Chief Instructor Tony Lanfranchi. He came across as very abrasive; he pointed to some stairs, saying to the viewing Gallery for the driver's

Briefing. We are going back a few years. The viewing Gallery would cross over the start-finish line giving great views around Indy Circuit. Instructors are milling around in and out of the race school cars along the pit lane. The Pupils looked like how I felt, nervous, with lots of meetings and greetings going on, thinking it would be me as soon as this briefing was over. About 15 Pupils were waiting for the briefing to begin, a short, grey-haired man in Blue and Red Brands Hatch Racing Overalls. He introduced himself as Les Aga, Chief Instructor. Compared with the briefings at the Speedway track, these were more professional, covering everything. He asked us if we had done any racing; I regrettably stuck my hand up and sad Speedway. He remarked he would expect a smooth drive from anyone who has raced a bike. Briefing over, we all waited to be called to the control tower by Tony Lanfranchi to be fitted with an open-faced helmet as we would have the test in a saloon car with a professional instructor sitting in the passenger seat, marking you out of 100%

Rick Shortle to the Control Tower please, my moment has arrived. I got fitted with a helmet and then told to go to car number 10; my instructor will be Les Aga, the chap that gave the briefing and having already met him, put me at ease.

Les remembered me from the briefing. He gave another in-car briefing and then asked me to drive out onto the track until we reached the bottom of Paddock Hill, the first corner. I did three laps, sticking to the rev limit. He then instructed me to go into the Pits and stop. He will finish his marking and then drive me for a fast lap around Brands. Les evaluates my drive. I did ok with a score of 84%, which was good enough to go out in a single-seater racing car.

Now it was the turn of the professional to show the standard I would require to reach if I wanted to race. Bugger, it's started raining; not sure if I would enjoy this. To me, it was more than exhilarating. I couldn't believe how fast these Pros drive; initially, I wondered if I could ever go like that. That put a smile on my face; now it's five laps in the FF1600. Back up to Tony Lanfranchi with my score sheet. Did you enjoy the fast lap with Les? I said not half; he said next time, we would put you out with someone quick. He told me to grab a full-faced helmet and go to single-seater number 4. I'm sure a youngster named Karl Boyo Jones was working with the single-seaters; what a driver he turned out to be; I've had the great pleasure of working with him. He was and still is one of the best saloon car drivers around. A briefing from the single-seater team, then out I go for my five laps with a rev limit, I think of 4500. rpm. I did the five laps, but I enjoyed the saloon more.

That was it; sadly, my day was over. or I thought it was, back up to see Tony Lanfranchi for a debrief. He explained that I could book the next session's intermediate class. You have 30mins one to one with an Instructor designed to improve your line and technique. Followed by five laps in the single-seater or ten laps in the saloon, I went for the ten laps with a raised rev limit of 5000. To get through, I had to reach or beat the set time. He said I could do that today, pop back to the office signing to book in, and, bugger it, why not. Once I got through the Advanced Class and completed the Class 1 test, I grabbed a pamphlet explaining. While driving around Brands Hatch Indi Circuit the opposite way in a single-seater with a time set by the great Tony Trimmer, I got to find out he was one hell of a driver.

I could enter the School races for £50, something I fancied doing. Within a couple of weeks, I passed the Advanced stage and the Class One Test, which meant I could enter the races in the school cars. Luckily the next School Race Meeting was only a few weeks away, so I hastily booked myself in.

At this point, Brother David and I kept up to speed with progress. He supported me for several years; he was my biggest critic and decided to come along and put in his twopenny worth. He sadly passed away some years later, but thankfully not until he watched me win. I miss him a lot.

The racing schools were so much better back in the day as they did their best to try and turn the pupils into race drivers, who worked for quite a few of us. I entered seven of the Brands Hatch saloon car races and was delighted with my performance. I won everyone. After each meeting, there was a presentation to the top three placed drivers. Presentation given by Brian Jones; I remember what he said when I won my first Race to this very day. The third-placed driver steps up for his cup, the second-placed driver steps for his cup, and then my turn for the first-placed cup. As I walked towards the podium for my cup, Brian Jones remarked that I was wearing my lucky, scruffy rugby shirt. We see the drivers looking like race drivers at this stage, except for Rick Shortle. I accepted the cup and then spoke, saying, I told my Brother David I wouldn't buy a suit until I win a race. David shouted; time to buy a race suit Bruv, great memory. Now I'm getting quite excited about the possibility of circuit racing in a car and not on a Bike. David and I discussed the next move as the school had done its job; the next step would be saloons or single-seaters, Formula Ford 1600.

# CHAPTER 6

## SINGLE SEATERS OR SALOONS?

I spoke with the BRSCC, the British Racing and Sports Car Club, based at Brands; they pointed me to the ff1600 route, saying that is the route to go down.

I got friendly with a chap who owned a Tiga ff1600; he hired out. It was a roll-up and race deal with no testing. I decided to do it; as a taster to see how I got on, I qualified last; out of 28 drivers, I finished 21st; a few drivers fell off during the Race, making it look better. My first ff1600 Race is all done and dusted. I didn't crash. I now realise racing isn't as easy as it seems. Our next step was to search and find ourselves an ff1600; BRSCC advised me to look in the Classified section of Autosport or Motoring News. These magazines will be my bible in the coming years.

We couldn't afford the latest model; the best funds would allow an older ff1600. We thought the best thing to scan through the Mag was to read about ff1600 drivers and what type of model they raced, which didn't help much. The winners were in the latest models, priced well out of our league.

We then looked in the ff1600 cars for sale to see what was available. One car that stood was a Royal RP21. Black looked good in the photo; the description of its history seemed ok. The owner is looking to buy a newer model. I called the owner to book a viewing for the following day; we took my plastering flatbed long wheelbase van just in case we decided to purchase. We purchased and were proud owners of a Royal RP21 ff1600 race car. We got it at a reasonable price as the engine needed a rebuild. They suggested I speak to Martin Spence of Auriga, one of the best engine builders. He gave me a ballpark guide for a rebuild, which seemed obscene; David felt he could find someone to rebuild it much cheaper than sending it to the engine builders.

The engines require rebuilding every 8 hours, which seemed to be no running time. However, I thought about the choices and decided to go to the professional. I spoke to Martin Spence and explained that I hadn't raced yet and knew nothing about racing. He said that was fine and suggested I deliver my engine to him to look at it and tell me more about cost etc. I did explain that the engine would be in a few pieces, but everything was there. I asked if it was OK to deliver it to him that day; he said yes, no problem.

We managed to get the engine out of the car, albeit in several pieces. I hadn't given much thought to how to get it to him. It wouldn't go in my car, so I put a dust sheet in a wheelbarrow and got a hand to lift the engine into it. Wrapping each piece separately to prevent loss or damage, I had a Morris 1000 van at the time; thankfully, it fitted in the back quite snugly. I made sure it was secure to stop it from rocking around. My journey from Ashford Kent to Auriga went well until we were within a spit away. We couldn't find Auriga. We thought it may have been a hoax. Luckily, a passerby directed us to Auriga, only a few hundred yards up a rough unmade road. I parked outside and asked a young guy if Martin Spence was around, I didn't know at the time, but that guy was the only Eddie Irvine. He was a genuinely unbelievable talent; he got to Formula One and teammate Michael Schumacher. I got to know Eddie quite well; Auriga sponsored him with their engines. Eddie went and found Martin. I introduced myself whilst pointing to the engine.

Martin then grabbed a couple of heavies to shoehorn the engine out the back of my Van. I never forgot the disbelief on all their faces, with a slight chuckle from Eddie Irvine. Martin Spence said he would look and get back to me; I explained the urgency as I was racing in a month. I got to know Eddie well, and we chatted a lot; if he wasn't racing, he was hanging out at Brands, and he never once mentioned the engine in the wheelbarrow.

They rebuilt the engine, and it was a perfect one. Thankfully David's friend put my rebuilt engine back in the RP21, ready for a test at Brands.

Buying the RP21 mirrored my purchase of the grass track bike; I didn't know what to do next; I felt like a headless chicken. I was so confused that I took David to Brands on a test day to help get started. I now own an ff1600, which I just about understand how to start up, not much else, baffled on how to go testing and racing.

We spent most of the day just watching the cars; they looked much faster than the race school 1600s. We spoke to some drivers, including Trevor Stiles and Karl Jones. Both were great guys and very helpful. I found out later that Trevor Stiles, known as Farmer Stiles, was a front-runner in the John Player ff1600 Champion of Brands series. At the time, Karl Jones, from Wales, was a mechanic for the Brands Hatch Racing School. He raced ff1600 and became one of the U.K.'s best Saloon car racers. They gave me lots of advice on testing and racing; I was beginning to feel a tad more relaxed. Little did I know, a few years later, I would be working alongside the Welsh Wizard on Car Manufacturer days all over the country, most of the USA. Circuits.

We spent the next few days organising a test day, sending away for a Novice race licence which would take 2 to 3 weeks to get issued; there was no online in those days, which was fine because there was also the issue of booking a test day, checking the RP21 over the best we could. Then rally around to get a toolbox, fuel cans etc.; yes, real grassroots stuff here, trying to do it cheaply. Before my first test session, I soon realised that motor racing wasn't affordable for a guy like me.

I still wanted to push on as I've always believed it would happen. If you wanted something enough, it would happen. Finally, our first test day arrived. The RP21 looked pretty good. Being black, I decided to put a few gold stripes down the sides, like the John Player Special Formula 1 Lotus. We arrived at Brands, the Paddock full of teams with race cars everywhere;

we never knew where you sign on. But once signed on, it all became more apparent. The chap in the signing-on office explained the format of the day. So here we are, all sorted and ready to go testing.

David and I did our best to prepare our car for some laps. A very good time for a lap in an ff1600 was a low 50 seconds. David was on the stopwatch, out I went, and Jesus, this was a baptism of fire, cars of all shapes and sizes, many so much quicker than us, change that too all cars were quicker than us. I did several laps; the next time, I noticed David beckoning me in over the start-finish line, so I came. I parked up, got out took my helmet off to see what Bruv had to say. David remarked, Rick, your best lap time was 56.1, nearly 6 seconds off a reasonable time. Thankfully I got more confident as the day went on. I did improve my lap time by some 2 seconds but still had 4 seconds to find. With this expensive rebuilt Auriga Engine, I was hoping to go quicker. Strangely enough, David seemed quite happy. I must admit to being knackered. We packed up and drove home to reflect on the day and discuss our way forward. If I booked it up as soon as possible, I would have another test before my first Race, which was in the John Player Special Champion of Brands ff1600 Series—getting excited now.

My first race is only a week away. Instructions for the meeting have arrived, and I see my name in the programme under John Player, Special Champion of Brand's drivers, Rick Shortle -RP21 - Ashford Kent. Having that roll-up and Race in the Tiga helped give us an idea of where to go on arrival. Then made our way to the competitor's Paddock. We looked for somewhere to park and found a spot next to a team They knew what they were doing. We got unloaded; I explained to the guys next to us that this was our first time. And we haven't got a clue. Would they mind advising? No problem was their reply. They helped us through the event, scrutiny, qualifying, and the Race. I found the whole day bloody stressful; without the help from our neighbours in the Paddock, I doubt we would have made it through the day. So did I enjoy it? Only the racing bit, I finished 24th out of 26. I didn't exactly set the world alight.

I had been spending far too much money on getting into motor racing. I was pissing against the wind. I gave it a lot of thought over the next few days and told David my decision to put the RP21 up for sale because I could never afford the expense of racing. He had a feeling; I may say that, said what a shame. I decided to sell the RP21 as a Rolling Chassis without the engine. As the engine had a rebuild, I would probably make more that way. I put it into the next issue of Autosport. Now I just had to wait for a response.

# CHAPTER 7

## ❖

# ENTER MARTIN DOWN OF GETEM GD RACING

I sat at the bottom of our stairs talking on the phone, probably about a plastering job. The conversation ended. Within a second or two, it rang again.

Is that Rick Shortle? to which I replied, how can I help? He then mentioned that he was the person we parked next to at Brands; Ken and I helped you out a bit; my name is Martin Down. Hi Martin, yes, you and Ken were a great help. What can I do for you? Martin remarked, " I see you have your Royal RP21 up for sale, and I hope you have not decided to pack in racing; you've just started." I went on to explain it was far too expensive. I certainly didn't want to stop, but I had no choice. He then explained that his driver Andy Best had decided to stop because his wife was pregnant and felt it was right. He then said that he (Martin) and Andy could see potential in me as a driver, even though they hadn't seen much of me apart from running as a backmarker. He then asked if I would be interested in coming to Brands for a test day in his ff1600. Martin built his car named the GETEM. All this was blowing my mind. If you think about it, I never had a bloody clue what I was doing, and then suddenly, by chance, I was offered to test Martins's GETEM ff1600. He told me to think about it and let him know soon as. I called Martin back that evening and said I would love to drive his car on a test day. He said that was fabulous and that he would get the ball rolling and call me with a test day date. I had to wait for Martin to contact me; he did the next day. I needed to be at Brands the following Wednesday and get there at 7.30 am to ensure I was comfortable in the GETEM. Martin went on to say, let's see how you get on, then we can have a chat afterwards.

So that was it. I was stunned, it hasn't sunk in yet, but I'm sure it will. I couldn't wait to tell Bro David. I explained it best I felt Martin might offer me a drive. David said, no chance; well, let us see, eh? I knew the test at Brands was so crucial that I had to impress in all areas. Martin said I would meet his right-hand man Ken Baker. Also, Andy Best would come along. Roll on next Wednesday.

I had to admit I was bloody useless over the next few days waiting for my big day at Brands, testing Martin Downs GETEM GD ff1600

# CHAPTER 8

## MY BIG DAY

I arrived at Brands at 6.30 am (I didn't want to be late). I've always been a good timekeeper. Bruv David was non too pleased with me picking him up at 5.30 am. It's a big day, Son. Well, I'm hoping and praying it will be.

Good job I got there early. Martin and Ken arrived shortly after us, and the first impression ticked. I jumped out of the car, shook hands with Martin and Ken, and then offered help. I must point out that David hasn't been in the best health for several years; he suffers from Spondylitis, which has left him with a curved spine. He uses a stick; there is no cure, and excruciatingly painful. Don't let David's appearance fool you. He's frightened of nothing and no one, it was fantastic having him along doing something he enjoys doing, so I put up with all his harsh remarks,

Anyway! Back to my Big Day, the car unloaded off the trailer and over to the pit lane area with Ken driving the Getem; we followed in our car Martin had booked a garage for the day. All was looking very professional. Martin backed his road car to the rear of the pit lane garages to unload tools. These guys were very organised and even had tea and coffee on hand. David is looking on using his shooting stick to rest his bum. I felt like a race driver for the first time, a lovely feeling.

Martin was excellent; he went through everything he was doing, explaining why. I signed on, got into my overalls, and wasn't used to sitting around and letting someone else do all the work. I whispered in

David's ear; what do you recon, he whispered back; you've just got to do the business now—grinning away with his smirk. Martin took me to scrutineering just as an exercise to show what goes on. We then put the Getem on the flatbed to check ride height. When I sat in the car, it felt completely different from any other ff1600; in a nutshell, it was very narrow; no problem, I am a skinny bugger.

Martin told me to stay in the car; he started it up; I then drove it back to the garage; it felt so bumpy as if it had no suspension and, to be honest, not very nice to drive; let's hope it's good at high speed. I told Martin I thought he explained race cars at low speeds are awful things to drive. Martin adjusted the mirrors, belts, etc. It was getting near time for the circuit to open for testing. I had instruction from Martin; he said to go out, keep out of the way of faster cars, do five laps, then come in; bloody hell, we had a pit board. I reported no problems; all dials were good, no overheating. Martin then said, go out; try to set a time without being silly. I was feeling fantastic.

My best lap time to date in my RP21 was 54.1, after six laps driving Martins Getem, I came in with a lap time of 52.4. Martin was pleasantly surprised; David was chuffed. Ken was Ken, always in shorts, always looking busy even if he wasn't; he's a lovely man; you will realise what a great asset he is as this book goes on. Out I went again, getting down to 51.8. We pit after six laps for lunch.

I've never felt so good in a race car; I can't stop smiling. After lunch, it was more of the same; Martin just wanted me to get used to driving his car; I was keen to improve my lap time. Each lap felt more comfortable throughout the day, certainly not the bumpy car I moved out of scrutiny this morning. I went for another six laps; I'm now beginning to feel confident. Overtaking slower cars was much more manageable, allowing me to keep up the rhythm

My lap time is up. Ken gave me the come in board. As I drove down the pit lane, Martin directed me into our garage. He told me to switch off and jump out. Helmet off, cuppa from Ken, Martin showed me all my lap times from the first lap out. David was earwigging too. My lap times improved every time I went out; my best time before lunch was 51.8. My six laps after lunch improved to 50.7. Martins driver Andy Best had turned up; we chatted, and he was amazed at my lap times.

I went again for another six laps, slightly disappointed that I could only knock a tenth off my lap time. Martin explained that the last second would be the hardest. He also remarked he never expected me to get anywhere near the time I did, and he would have been happy with a 52.00. Martin asked me if I minded Andy doing a few laps; I was more than happy; I wondered how quick he would be.

Andy completed a dozen laps but couldn't beat my best time; his best time was a tenth slower than mine. I was ecstatic. Andy didn't seem upset; he seemed very happy because Martin had found himself a suitable replacement driver. We had a good chat; he wished me luck, said his goodbyes, and left. Sadly we had run out of time—what a fabulous day, and a day that may hopefully help me become a decent race driver; fingers crossed.

We helped load up; Martin said, let's go to the Kentigon for a cuppa and a chat. I was hoping I had done enough to impress Martin and Ken that they would offer me to run on their team.

David said I did a great job, and GETEM GD RACING is a good team. In the Kentigon, we had a cuppa; Martin opened the discussion with praise for the way I drove and the lap time I reached. He went on to explain GETEM GD RACING's history. Martin built a new car each year or redesigned his last year's chassis. He then made an offer. Suppose I agreed to put what I got for the RP21 into the pot to fund next year, allowing me to race at most of the circuits in the U.K. It will help me get used to racing an ff1600 and driving the circuits to prepare for the 1983 Dunlop Autosport Star of Tomorrow Championship. Martin explained his ambitions, one of them was to win a race in his GETEM GD ff1600. Well, wouldn't that be fabulous?

I agreed with Martins's offer there and then, telling Martin that I wanted to learn as much as possible and that I would travel to Martins to help in any way, shape or form. Martin and Ken were delighted. They both got up and remarked that the GETEM TEAM are known for their hugs, so let's seal the deal with a GETEM hug. We did, and the hugs from then on were a standard part of our day. We said our goodbyes; Martin said he would call me in a day or two with a going-forward plan, so home to Ashford for David and me. Martin and Ken are just up the road to Hartley Dartford, three miles from Brands. What a day! To think that phone call from Martin Down changed everything; I could quite quickly have sold the RP21 and then called it a day; thanks, Martin.

I haven't seen Bro David so upbeat for a long time which was a great feeling; being in constant pain like he is must be awful. Hopefully, this will give him something to focus on and make things more bearable. I'm more than prepared to let him criticise; it's his way of giving me advice; he must be so frustrated, not being able to have a go himself. I couldn't describe how I felt at that moment; I couldn't tell; it was disbelief how things had changed in such a short time; I still didn't know what was in store. It was hard to imagine racing in a championship that would take us all over England. The next couple of days waiting for Martin to call seemed like forever. I was getting funny thoughts like, has he changed his mind?

I read in Autosport that there was a big meeting at Brands this coming weekend at the Formula Ford Festival. Bruv was up for that, so off we went. It was a three-day meeting, but I decided only on Sunday as finals day. We arrived at the main gates of the circuit, purchased two tickets and a programme, and then made our way to the parking areas; the whole place was buzzing with the sound of ff1600 racing; I was getting impatient and wanted to get trackside to see ff1600.

Now for the Racing. We chose to observe at the exit of Paddock Hill Bend just in time to see the start of another race. I quickly checked the Programme for drivers; we didn't know any names. In this race were Rick Morris and 28 other drivers; as the lights changed, this roar of ff1600's was heading into Paddock Hill Bend, amazing-like gladiators fighting for a position; it was exciting-dangerous and fantastic. I couldn't wait; even David said fucking hell, Rick, getting to that standard will be tough. I just said I couldn't wait, but to be honest, I knew it was going to be a challenge. After watching the race, which Rick Morris won(I thought he was terrific), I also watched another chap from Brazil, a certain Ayrton Senna; I never heard of him but certainly know who he is now, also a James Weaver and Tommy Byrne; I've read his book crash and Byrne. I followed Rick Morris through his heats, quarter, semi, and final. Where he made the podium, losing to Senna and James Weaver. Since that day, Rick Morris has been the driver I genuinely respected. He was and still is one of the best drivers out there. Over the years, I've often walked past Rick, and I would say hi to Rick, and he always politely replied, it sounds daft. Even though I had been racing for several years, I still got a kick out of saying hi to Rick; I was like a spectator, feeling chuffed about him acknowledging me. Silly sod.

Years later, at the Silverstone 2021 Walter Hayes Formula Ford Championship weekend. I happened to bump into Rick; I said Hi; Rick shook his hand, then said, I'm Rick Shortle, I replied I know who you are, and I can honestly say I've never been more chuffed about anything; we had a great chat, for the very first time. Mega.

# CHAPTER 9

# A CALL FROM GETEM GD RACING

The phone rang, it was Martin with his usual answer. "Hello there, how are youhooo." Make sure you've had your dinner when Martin rings because it's usually a marathon call. I was so excited and nervous simultaneously; talking to Martin Down, the ff1600 builder of his car named the "GETEM GD", I could feel myself talking at 100 mph and getting my words wrong. Slowly, the conversation became more straightforward; it wasn't long before we both seemed to get on like a house on fire. I didn't want this first conversation about racing to stop; racing speedway was now well into the back of my mind. Martin suggested I come to the Workshop to meet his wife, Judy. Then go through the plans for the next couple of years—I.E., 1982, a year of learning, then the 1983 Dunlop Autosport Star of Tomorrow Championship.

Martin has an excellent job with ESSO; he works five days a week and can take time off to travel mid-week. I work as a self-employed plasterer; committing to any mid-week testing required is certainly ok. My first visit to Martins was mid-week; I knocked on the door; Judy, his wife, answered, and a lovely lady who talked very posh; I hope I wasn't too shocked. Judy invited me in and offered me a cup of tea, Earl grey; it had to be, I accepted, not owning up to the fact I was not too fond of the stuff. It wasn't long before Martin arrived, all suited and booted; I wasn't expecting that. We all chatted away. Martin got changed, and then off we went to the top of the garden. I could see a good-sized garage; we entered through a side door from the garden. There, in all its glory, was Martins GETEM sitting on stands. The garage was very tidy, with a place for everything; I was excited; Martin invited me to put on a pair of overalls. We spent all that evening just chatting. He plans to develop me as a driver and make changes to the car, giving it the opportunity to go even quicker. I was so amazed and even more gobsmacked that I was in a situation like this when I was about to chuck in the towel less than a month ago.

I asked Martin if I could pop up and help out, I am practical, and as long as he explains what he would like me to do, it should be ok. Martin was over the moon and said Ken didn't visit the garage too much; he preferred the racing side of things. He's a bloody good problem solver. We nicknamed him just a thought, Ken. Although a lovely chap, Ken can be, at times, infuriating. Over the coming years, Bruv David got on well with Ken; in a way, they were like peas in a pod, a couple of wind-up merchants. After chatting all evening, I was about to leave for home when Ken arrived; needless to say, it was very late before I got home, but worth it as I got to learn more about Ken.

Back home, I worked on the tools five days a week as a plasterer, and before too long, I would also be travelling to Martins evenings, Monday to Friday. When I think about it now, Anne was marvellous to allow me to do this. For which I apologise. It was bloody selfish of me!! That I know now. I was so passionate and determined to be a decent race driver that nothing else mattered. Yes, I got the bug; I wasn't someone with wealthy parents; if I wanted to succeed, there was only one way, the hard way. I've always said if you want something that much, don't give up. It will happen.

So now I'm looking to the future with the knowledge I have a small team, "GETEM GD RACING", looking after me. I want to repay them with good results, hopefully sometimes with a win or two.

# CHAPTER 10

## TRYING TO RAISE SPONSORSHIP

It was the end of the 1981 race season; Martin had the winter to redesign his car, ready for my first year in an ff1600, I can't wait. Apart from travelling to Martins every evening, I began to think of ways to get sponsorship; my thoughts of being sponsored by Brian and Celia Elma from the ABC STORES whilst I rode Speedway inspired me to try.

If there is one thing I'm good at, it's selling myself first, then selling a product I believe in, which has always been the key. Being a plasterer, I worked for all kinds of people. If I could, without ramming it down their throats when I talk to my customers, try to bring into the conversation that I raced ff1600 and looking for sponsorship, most weren't interested. However, the odd one did. So I forwarded them the details. Another idea I came up with was to use my work van, a red Morris 1000, as an advertising hoarding, I.E., around the outside of the roof rack; I fixed boards as advertising spaces. Two to each side and one board to the back and front. I quickly sold two spaces to "The Newchurch House Restaurant" from Ivy Church New Romney and a company called Cosy Burn from Hythe.

So I then decided To tow GETEM GD RACING's ff1600 behind my Van and simply cold call businesses. It shows them the race car and the advertising spaces on the Van with a couple of companies already signed up, and it may hopefully generate some interest. Within no time at all, I managed to sell all six spaces. I never made a fortune, and it was a start; It worked out that each advertising space would buy a tyre.

Martin was delighted with my efforts; it was another sign that I was serious. I quickly learned the importance of awareness, selling myself, and promoting the product. I continued talking to people hoping a few more would show interest; I had to wait patiently. Meanwhile, I continued plastering during the day, gulping down my evening meal, then driving from Sellindge near Folkestone to Martins in Hartley Dartford. About a sixty-mile journey in total.

It was January 1982; the revised GETEM showed signs of getting near completion. Martin even started talking about getting out for a test day at the end of February, weather permitting. I can't wait. I travelled to the GETEM workshop, enjoyed the tasks, and learned more about the GETEM ff1600 every visit. Most importantly, Martin and I were bonding, proving its worth over the next few years; we had tremendous belief and respect in each other. I continued looking for sponsorship; I got a plastering job in a lovely old house that straddled a stream in Wye Nr Ashford Kent, owned by a chap named Johnny Weir. He had a medium-sized business in Ashford called The Ashford Accident and Repair Centre. As usual, we got chatting. I waited until I could mention my racing; he was very interested, saying he had already sponsored someone in another formula. Johnny asked if I needed spraying on the car chassis, suspension, etc. He would do that as a sponsorship deal, FOC., but then he said he knows someone who could be interested. He loves cars but is a very cautious chap, a bit of a slow burner; I will have a word with him.

I was over the moon, so I called Martin and told him about Johnny Wier; he was delighted; at least this saved Martin from having to paint the chassis himself...It wasn't long before Ashford Accident Repair Centre painted quite a bit for Getem GD Racing. They did a fantastic job, and it felt great bringing more to the table. Over the coming years, Johnnies Company did a lot for us, ie. powder coating the new chassis, spraying the suspension and bodywork, which proved a great help—allowing Martin to get on with other things.

# CHAPTER 11

## MY FIRST OUTING IN THE GETEM GD112

It's now early February; the revised Getem is nearing completion. I enjoyed sitting in the car whilst Martin adjusted the pedals, steering, and gear shift. Boy, did I feel important? Bloody right, I did. I'm so so fortunate with the 1982 " GD112" Getem. We spent hours discussing everything; Martin gave me the Formula Ford book by Nick Brittan, hoping it could help. What a leap of faith for Martin Down and a journey into the unknown for myself. Martin booked our first test for the end of February at Brands Hatch, weather permitting. It's not long to wait now. The test at Brands did go ahead; the weather for the end of February wasn't that bad, albeit it was a tad cold. I was pretty nervous. Bruv David came to support; Martin was as calm and quiet-spoken as ever. He never used two words if one would do. Just a thought, Ken Baker carried out his duties, including tea-making, problem-solving and being an all-around good egg. I haven't mentioned myself, for I still have to prove myself.

So this is all systems go; the GD112 is running, Martin and Ken check for leaks, etc., had my briefing from Martin. Ken shuts down the engine. I slide into the cockpit of the GD112, feeling equally excited and nervous; I give Martin the sign to start the car, and the engine roars. I am waiting for Ken to usher me out of the garage, ready to drive down the pit lane and onto the track. All clear to join the circuit; now, my head seems full of a thousand feelings. It takes me a lap or two to settle down. I remember Martin advising me to take it easy, keep out of the way, do a couple of laps, and then come in so they could check the car over. I was so pleased to pit. I wasn't feeling confident; I told Martin, who said not to worry. Please don't feel pressured; he gave me the famous Getem Hug, which did the trick. Out I went, I felt great, the car felt good; this time, I was enjoying myself and ready for the day ahead. We had a fab day; I thoroughly enjoyed driving the GETEM ff1600. It felt so different, a good race car, and so pleased to have improved my lap times, but most of all, settled in with the small but perfectly formed team.

# CHAPTER 12

## 1982 A LEARNING YEAR

I admit that apart from knowing where Brands Hatch and Silverstone were, I knew bugger all about the other circuits. I, of course, checked out their location to find we would be travelling the length and breadth of the country. Martin suggested the following circuits, Thruxton, Castle Coombe, Brands Hatch, Silverstone, Mallory Park, Donington,Cadwell Park, Oulton Park and Croft. Nine circuits in all.

Thank goodness the funds I received from selling my race car will pay for most of the season. Providing I don't have too many expensive accidents would certainly dent the wallet. I will have to continue to raise sponsorship as best I can. Being a small team, "GETEM GD RACING" can cut down the cost of racing. Everything made in the Workshop is a labour of love, so that's free; I would religiously go to Martin's 5 evenings a week to help in any way I could. I loved the whole experience, something I will cherish for the rest of my life.

Our first outing of 1982 was to Thruxton. At 4 am it was a cold frosty morning. As we set off, the journey seemed to go on forever; not to worry, we were all upbeat and looking forward to the test day. Our first outing was not for a race, just another day of testing as Martin felt it a good idea, so Thruxton was the only one open for testing. Martin wanted to see how I would fare on a circuit I've never been to; after all, I have done quite a few miles at Brands, if you include the Racing School. We finally arrived at Thruxton, utterly different to Brands, I first noticed that you couldn't see much of the track, unlike Brands, where you could watch and see most of the Indi Circuit.

As we pulled up with our trailer behind, I started to feel nervous; a fair share of the Paddock had lorries and transporters parked up. Drivers had already suited up; I didn't know who they were. Martin parked, and we all shared duties to unload the race car and set it up for the test day. I'm grateful to have something to do as I feel like a new Boys first day at school. Martin noticed a few people were driving very slowly around the circuit in their road cars; Ken's first job was to find out who we had to see to do the same. David got in the back with Ken; I asked Martin if I could drive he said yes. So there we were, a new one to me but fascinating. The first thing we thought, compared to Brands, Thruxton was a more comprehensive, longer, fast circuit slowed down by a chicane just before the finish line, then a complex Cambell Cobb and Segrave. I can't wait to get out there now. There was quite a bit of fog and mist, particularly at the chicane. It was pretty challenging to see through that section, something to remember when I get out there.

We had a while before the circuit was open; our car was ready, Ken made a cuppa and Martin asked me if I would like to tour the Paddock to look at the other ff1600. We soon spotted a few, particularly the Works Van Dieman's yellow and blue colours. Martin pointed out the drivers, telling me their names and country; several different manufacturers of ff1600, Royal, Sark, Ray, Swift. Eldon and, of course, the Getem driven by Rick Shortle. After an exciting couple of laps of Thruxton in our road car, we got the Chequered flag, so in we came. I needed to get into my race gear; now, I don't have a helmet, so I use the Getem team helmet; not the prettiest one, but it will certainly do. The Paddock comes alive with engines warming up; it's not long before the circuit is open for practice. I'm shaking, not with cold now; I reckon it was nerves.

It seemed forever before I got into the cockpit of the 112; happily, my shaking stopped. We are now in the pit lane, ready to go onto the track. A Marshall blows his whistle and waves his green flag; we all go. Luckily I'm last out which gives me time to settle in; I remember shouting out as

I exit Segrave "bloody hell, this is fabulous". This next bit is hilarious. As I approached the chicane, the fog/mist had gotten worse. I couldn't see a bloody thing. Back in the day, there was a service road just before the entry of the chicane. It took you down the side of a grandstand and ended up in a car parking area. Yes, you guessed it, that's where I ended up, well away from the circuit and not having completed one lap. I didn't know what to do next; I just had to hope our knight in shining armour; just a thought Ken Baker would appear through the mist; it wasn't long before he did. Ken organised a circuit breakdown truck to pick the Getem up and take it back to our spot in the Paddock. I got a lift back in the breakdown truck and felt the curious eyes of other teams and drivers. However, it's something drivers get used to during their time as race drivers. Felt quite embarrassed as I returned to the pits. Martin greeted me with one of his famous Team hugs. I felt good and ready to go. He would always come to me first if I had an off or worse, to see if I was ok. Before too long, I felt part of the TEAM.

I got to chat with Eddie Irvine, the Works Driver for Van Diemen, which gave me a boost. It wasn't a bad day for testing, and I improved my lap times, but I am not brilliant compared to Eddie Irvine. I was reasonably happy with my first day of testing on a track that was new to me. I loved the journey home, Martin driving, Ken in the front seat and myself in the back with my Brother David. Martins's choice of tow car was an Austin Princess. He swore by this model for plenty of room, comfort, and, well, not everybody's choice, but it never let us down. The journey home was long but enjoyable, non stop talking about the day. It was so good racing with Getem's total commitment from Martin, and just a thought, Ken with Brother David getting involved. For me, this was day one of living, thinking, breathing and becoming a race driver.

I didn't seem to achieve much as a driver that day; to me, we gained the most important thing. As one, we were a Team. from that day forward. I lived, ate and breathed motor racing.My Life changed from this day onward; I could think of nothing other than racing a formula ford

1600—the Getem ff1600. I was still a full-time plasterer. I thought of nothing else than driving the race car and looking forward to my evening journey to help Martin in his Workshop at New Ash Green. I wanted to be a competitive race driver, a race winner.

# CHAPTER 13

## THE LEARNING YEAR BEGINS

The excitement, expectations and thought of travelling to the U.K.'s premier race circuits filled my head. It was late February 82, Martin booked the races and testing, and we were ready to go. I'm not going to give you a report of how I got on in testing and the races; instead, here's a brief rundown of how it went.

I always did well in testing, never the quickest but always in the top six to ten drivers. My main problem was driving beyond my ability, so spinning off was regular. Martin did his best to calm me down, although he seemed happy for me to carry on, hoping it would all come together sooner rather than later.

I got a bit of a stick from David; it was frustrating for him throughout this year. As I mentioned earlier, he would love a go if he were fitter. The races were a massive learning curve. Out of the 14 races entered, I only managed to finish in 50% of them and nine times out of ten, we had to take a damaged GETEM race car home, so there was plenty of work for us to do back at the New Ash Green workshop.

I didn't achieve any good results, but the odd one or two races showed promise. Martin was excellent; he stayed his usual quiet self, hopefully, he could see more in me than I could at the time. I was a little disillusioned with my progress by the end of that first year. I told Martin how I was feeling, and with that, he nipped down to his house and returned with a book; it was an Alain Prost book about his early years as a race driver; Martin gave me the book to read. I read the book; Alain had many accidents in his early years as a race driver. Alain explained that if you don't have offs, you are just not trying hard enough; if you do, then great, because you are overdriving and will find the limits of yourself and the car. Great words of wisdom; I felt good after reading this book and couldn't wait to get back into the GETEM ff1600.

My first year of racing ff1600 was now run, and Martin already had the new GETEM GD113 on the drawing board, including drawings of the new look bodywork. The GETEM bodywork up to then used skinny aviation plywood. Every other marque used glass fibre, and I questioned Martin why he was different, his simple answer was quicker, easier and cheaper. He then said he thought I would have the skills to make a nose cone out of glass fibre because I was a plasterer. I read up on how to do this; Martin was right. I should produce a nose cone by forming a plug and then a mould to have the finished item. The only worry would be the cost of the materials. Again by chance, in the Town of Ashford, just down the road from me, was a company named Strand Glass Fibre Products, and by chance, I knew the Manager. So next day off, I popped in to say hello, I explained what I wanted to do and wondered if he would supply us with materials to carry out the work. He was very interested and asked his boss for a sponsorship deal.

The Manager put me on the phone to talk with his boss. He was a great bloke who loved the idea of having the company name on the race car. He was happy with our chat and said he couldn't give me funds but would supply me with all the material and advice to make bodywork; he also included overalls for the GETEM TEAM. I called Martin and gave him the news. I suggested to Martin that we make a complete set of bodywork; he thought it would be a great idea. So new bodywork, here we come. I had until February to make the bodywork ready to put on the car. Exciting.

# CHAPTER 14

## THE 1983 DUNLOP AUTOSPORT STAR OF TOMORROW CHAMPIONSHIP

We all put in so many hours over the winter months to ensure the car was ready; there were times when I wondered if it would be. Thankfully the GETEM GD113 was complete with stunning new bodywork designed around a front radiator. Martin had booked a day of testing at Brands as the first round of the championship was there. Also, our home circuit is down the road from Martins's workshop in New Ash Green. It will be exciting to meet with the drivers and teams and understand how I fair against some 28 drivers. Test day was here. I arrived at a paddock full of ff1600. Was I excited? Yes, was I nervous? Yes. I found my way to TEAM GETEM. I thought I was early; Martin and Ken were already there and ready to go. After the Team hug, it was time for a cup of tea, a chat about the car, and plans for the day's testing.

Brother David was sitting on his shooting stick, taking it all in. Although his remarks never had a filter, It was great to have him around. My initial worry was the inconsistency of my driving, as last year was a bit of a demolition derby, ie, only finishing 50% of the races, damaging the car more often than not. I wanted to improve on last year and hopefully get a couple of top-ten finishes.

The Paddock was a fantastic spectacle, with so many ff1600's under awnings. One that sticks in my mind is the Van Dieman of the one and only Perry McCarthy, his car looking mega adorning his sponsor Lee

Cooper; I wondered if that was his sponsor or if a bit of kidology from Perry, I might ask him one of these days.

Another was the Red Ray, driven by Johnny Robinson. Johnny was tipped for top honours in this championship, as were several other drivers. If I remember correctly, the weather was dry and overcast. It was time for teams to fire up their steeds; the almost silent Paddock began to roar

Activity quickly built up across the entire Paddock. Most drivers were suited booted and sliding into their formula fords. I don't know what it was, but I was trembling, hopefully with excitement. I relied on Ken and Martin to advise me on what to do next; it worked well for me.

The day's testing went well; my lap times put me in the top five; I was delighted with that as it was on the Grand Prix Circuit and I had never been on it before. We ran without any dramas. The GETEM performed without a hiccup, and more importantly, so did the driver, a certain Rick Shortle. My first day was so enjoyable. I felt much more at home than last year; I can't describe how I felt. Whatever it was, I was feeling great. I am looking forward to the first Race of The Dunlop Autosport Star of Tomorrow Championship at Brands, Round One, this coming weekend.

So back to Martins for a debrief! All happy, including David, I was buzzing and chuffed, feeling as if I had gone through a barrier but couldn't put my finger on it apart from the fact I felt in control and that I was part of the car; that's it, I was part of the car. Roll on the Race.

Race day. I qualified 4th behind the late great Peter Rogers, which put me on the second row; I was happy with that. Back on the day, Brands was a three on the front row, two on the second row etc., later altered to a two-two grid due to some awful coming together at the start.

The Race. I admit to being somewhat nervous and excited while happy with my position on inside of row two. I planned to make a good start, hugging tight on entry through Paddock, hopefully doing the same up to and around the Druids Hairpin. It was fantastic to see the circuit ahead, with only the front row blocking me from a perfect view of the first corner

Paddock. What an improvement from last year. I was back on row ten or eleven; then all I could see ahead was 20 or so cars most of the time. I made a decent start and stuck to my plan. It worked but was bloody hectic; that's ff1600. Rogers was behind. I had managed to get up to third with Rogers right up my chuff. Sadly Peter Rogers had to retire. I could see the leaders. Horwood /Robinson are having a ding don battle, allowing me to catch them. I think Horwood made a mistake allowing Robinson through. I can't remember where I overtook both Johnny Robinson and Horwood, but I led the first round of the championship. It was fabulous; I just needed to stay ahead and take the chequered flag as the winner and Championship leader. I punched the air so hard, it was so emotional I had tears in my eyes. I crossed the start-finish line to take the chequered flag, my first win in ff1600 in the GETEM GD 113. I couldn't wait to return to Martin Down, Ken Baker and Brother David.

The winners' cars would park on the start-finish line on those days. Once out of the car, you would walk to the commentary tower and nine times out of ten, the winner would be greeted by non-other than Brian Jones, the voice of Brands Hatch, the very Man who ran Motor Racing Stables and was my first port of call when I decided to become a race driver, and what a good advert one of their pupils winning his first race in only his second year of racing. I enjoyed being interviewed by Brian Jones and boy, did I enjoy my lap of honour on the back of the course car, complete with my garland? Dam right, I did.

As I hopped off the course car, I could see Martin, Ken and Brother David waiting to greet me; I went straight to Martin for a Team hug and whispered in his ear, here's the win you craved for, hopefully, the first of many. What a start to the year; being realistic, there's a long way to go, but I'm at the sharp end; things are looking good. Back to Martin's for a debrief. It's great having a debrief when we've done so well. Unlike last year, a big Brucie Bonus is a race car in one piece. Martin was already thinking of improving the car. Over the coming years, we would try out all sorts of outrageous things, many of which were of no benefit so we went back to the initial set-up. I soon realised that testing wasn't about going around in circles all day. I loved testing.

Round two at Silverstone. We did an ok weekend with a top 6 finish. But the highlight was meeting Formula One driver Alan Jones; he was filming grassroots racing and exciting cars, which the GETEM certainly was. I was bloody nervous when he asked if it was ok to interview me, he then interviewed Martin, who was much more experience than me at being interviewed It seems that in motor racing, exciting things happen not only in the Race.

I was competitive, top three or four, but felt we lacked straight-line speed; Martin thought we should go to a side radiator instead of the existing front radiator, which could have caused drag and speed loss. He asked if I would like to have a go and revise the bodywork; it was a big yes from me; it should be easier this time as all I needed to do was re-gig the existing plug and mould. I had three weeks to turn it out, a big order, so best get on with it. Get on with it I did; I just about got it ready in time to test before the next round at Castle Combe. Martin was correct. We stayed in the top three in testing, but our times were much closer to the drivers in first and second, Robinson and McCarthy. I Qualified 3$^{rd}$ as predicted and should have had a top-three finish in the Race, the team's first retirement due to a gearbox jam. Oh well, that's motor racing, as they say. The revised bodywork did the trick; the new shape looked the business.

If I remember correctly, Martin and Kens Boys came along; it's always hilarious when they do. In particular, for Ken and his Boys, Bedtime was so funny; they had to get in their P.J.'s. Ken would put a hat on and sleep with his head outside the tent; David reminded him a dog could come along and cock his leg up.

I was so relieved that no major damage had been done to the car. My driving had improved, meaning there was only the jammed gearbox to deal with.and Martin could fix that. However I was desperately trying to raise more sponsorship. I decided to cold call a few big stores in Ashford, Kent. One, in particular, was a furniture store; by the name of Bassetts. I took some blurb along. I waited patiently to speak to the gentleman that was busy at that time. After a while, he said, hi, I'm Russell. How can I help? I explained that I was looking for sponsorship and wondered if it would interest his business; he immediately showed interest, telling me he was a big Formula One Fan. Russell loves a chat and we talked for ages; it was one of those by-chance situations; I walked out of there with some sponsorship. Russell has been a sponsor and friend since 1983, he sponsored me until I hung my helmet up, and since then, I have introduced him to a couple of drivers. I mentor, Matt Luff and Ben Powney. Interestingly, Russell now sponsors Matt and Ben.

About a week later, I had a call from Brian Varney, the Legal Service chap. He invited me to come and see him in his office as he would like to discuss additional sponsorship. Off I went wondering what amount of support he was going to offer. Brian is very professional and does everything to the letter. To cut a long story short, Brian said he has been following my progress and was impressed. Therefore, he wanted to be the main sponsor, handle all bills, etc. Brian put together a Star of the Eighties brochure, distributed to business associates to generate further funding. He soon got in touch with the local press, sending them regular press releases and more that helped me go motor racing. Brians's input over the years has been invaluable, for which I was and still am incredibly grateful. However, with a sponsor such as Brian Varney that invests a lot of money into their driver, the driver is under a different pressure to do well, ie win races and be approachable to sponsors, friends, and associates.

The last couple of years were nail-biting stuff money-wise, not knowing if I could manage. But now, I have a significant sponsor, Brian Varney Legal Services. Within a few weeks, I had won my first race, led the championship, and secured a major sponsor; please don't wake me up if I'm dreaming. I couldn't get my head around how this would happen. However, it soon became apparent. I get on with the racing, look after my sponsors, and let everything else take its course. Bloody hell. I can race without worrying. I called to let Martin know! he was very happy for me. I still went to Martins every night to help out and chat about racing; I loved it.

Racing was far less worrying; I could slide into my GETEM113 and focus on the job. Although I didn't win this championship, I finished third behind Perry McCarthy and Johnny Robinson. It's worth mentioning I finished every Race apart from Castle Combe's retired Gearbox jam. 100% better than the year before.

Martin invited Brian to the Workshop over the winter period as a bonding exercise, which went very well. We agreed on plans for 1984. It was either the National Championship or the John Player Special Champion of Brands; We decided on the John player C.O.B. Brian wanted Brands because it was ideal for him to attend every Race and organise Hospitality overlooking the Indi circuit. Blimey, it looks like people will be coming to watch. Brian was now very much involved, so we kept him up to speed.

The engine was due for a rebuild; it required a rebuild every 8 hours. During the summer, Minister engine builder's Sales Manager, Graham Fuller courted us, they wanted front runners to use their engines. Martin got on well with Dave Minister, owner and tuner of Minister, so we decided to switch.

# CHAPTER 15

## UNEXPECTED

In early 1984 I received a letter from Brands Hatch owner John Webb; who also owned Snetterton, Oulton Park and Cadwell Park. He invited me to go and see him for a chat. Intrigued, I met him in the Kentagon Bar / Restaurant at Brands. John would always perch himself on a stool at the far end of the Bar. Bearing in mind that I'd never met him, we shook hands. John told me I was becoming a good ff1600 racer so would I like to be a race instructor? John went on to say that because I've come through the Race School and won races,it would be good for the school to use in their publicity. Making me a Race Instructor would show that the school produces decent race drivers.

Back then race drivers required an invitation to become instructors; I was amazed and chuffed to bits at the invite. As an Instructor, back then you certainly earned your salt; it was serious stuff; it was a race school, not a place where you come along for a bit of fun, as it is today. I accepted the offer to become an instructor but needed time to sort out my plastering jobs before committing to dates with Brands Hatch Racing School. John Webb was happy to wait. What a whirlwind time I'm having; long may it last. More about being an instructor etc., later.

# CHAPTER 16

## 1984 FF1600 JOHN PLAYER SPECIAL CHAMPION OF BRANDS

1984, and I will soon be able to put Race Instructor Brands Hatch Racing on my resume; I still cannot believe it was only four years ago I was a pupil at the same school.

Martin felt the GD113 chassis worked well and would still be competitive apart from some tweaks which included changing to inboard suspension. I was looking forward to getting out in the GETEM GD114 to feel the difference.

During the winter, Martin trained me to weld to produce parts under his supervision; of course, everything I did for Martin also allowed me to understand the workings of a single seat race car. Thanks to Strand Glass Fibre, I could sheet out the sides of the trailer, making it look professional with the Sponsor's names etc adorning the sides.

I was looking forward to contesting a full year of the "C.O.B" (Champion of Brands). I would be racing against the regular contender's drivers and Brands specialists, such as Chris Hall in the Jamun, John Oxborrow in the unique OX, and Farmer Trevor Styles in his multi-starred livery, Van Diemen. Chris Cresswell and Chris Ringrose in their black and white Rays, Glen Board in the latest Van Diemen, Len Bull, Van Diemen, Colin Stancombe in a Lola, etc etc. are all capable of winning the championship. I'm looking forward to the challenge. With an excellent year in 1983, contesting the Dunlop Autosport Star of Tomorrow and finishing third, we were looking forward to doing the John Player Special, ff1600 Champion of Brands, my home circuit. Going to the Workshop was so enjoyable, plus it helped keep the cost down. Martin did it for his love of the sport, seeing his self-built race car Win races and see the racing fraternity sit up and notice what a genius he is.

The 1984 season is fast approaching. Our car is ready to get its first run. Brands; here we come, just ten minutes down the road from Martin's Workshop.

I am proud to be part of a small but highly professional team; the car and revised trailer looked like the business, parked at the rear of the pit garages. It was late February, and we were praying for the weather to stay mild as we had booked a test day for the last week of the month. Thankfully, it stayed mild; it was good to see so many of the C.O.B drivers present; this would give us an idea of how good the car is and how my lap times fared against my competitors.

To begin with, it was a baptism of fire. These regular Brands specialists certainly know their way around this track. As expected, I was initially slightly off the pace, dipping into the top ten out of thirty drivers. Martin was more than pleased; he gave me strict instructions to drive well within myself in the first session as he needed to check everything was working ok. The first session is over, not back out for another hour, so Ken makes tea, David his usual quiet self, resting on his shooting stick, waiting to pounce with a remark, excellent or bad. The GETEM114 performed without a hiccup; by the end of the day, my times were in the top five; at one stage, I was quickest, but not for long. We were all happy with that; I'm new to this highly competitive championship; it's a long season! Twenty-three races from the 4th of March to the 2nd of December. A lot can happen over so many races. I didn't know many drivers; I said Hi to Farmer Trevor Styles and Karl Jones. Here's hoping I will get to know more in the coming months.

That's the end of the first test of 1984, as the car was still in one piece and behaved well. We packed away, had a debrief in the Kentagon, and said our goodbyes. David and I made our way to Ashford Kent, and Martin and Ken set off on their ten-minute drive to the Workshop. After a good drive home, Bro David was suitably happy. We need to trim a bit off my lap times; I reckon four-tenths should get me on the second row. Let's see; the first Race is on the 4th of March.

Race day has arrived. In round one of the "1984 C.O.B" I was very nervous, which was good. I was the same throughout my whole racing career; I used to scuttle off to my road car, recline the seat, have a bit of shut-eye, then I was ready to wander back to the team and prepare for qualifying or the Race.

Qualifying. Back then, you had to park in a collection area before driving down and through the tunnel to get to the pits or grid. Martin explained the importance of getting out for qualifying, we needed to line up in the collection area before anyone else, which we achieved 99% of the time. First, qualifying for C.O.B. was tough, and I qualified a disappointing 10th. So there was work to do in the Race.

Race 1. Wow, it was no-holds-barred racing. In a way, I was pleased to be back in tenth; I could watch the front runners; it demonstrated how good these drivers were, knowing that I still had work to do if I wanted to be upfront. I did have something to smile about; I managed to detach myself from the chasing pack to secure the fastest lap as the only driver to break 50secs with an eighth-place finish.

Race 2. This one mirrored Race One, I was quick! The GETEM was fabulous to drive. I kept getting the fastest lap in the race but needed time to learn racecraft. These boys were top draw, better put my thinking cap on. Martin was very pleased with me; I found our chats helped.

Race 3. I qualified 2nd, the middle of the front row, with Len Greenery and Chris Ringrose either side of me. My Getem 114 is certainly showing promise, only the Race will tell. The start went well, I managed to out drag Greenery and Ringrose which gave me the opportunity to dip into the first corner Paddock Hill Bend in the lead. This allowed me to command the race and as long as I am first into the Hairpin Druids I have a great chance of controlling the race. We were on the Grand Prix Circuit, it would be great if I win, as I won on the GP Circuit last year in the Dunlop Autosport Star of Tomorrow Championship. Apparently all hell was let loose behind me which at the time I wasn't aware of, I got my head down, bringing our 114 home to another victory.

Race 4. I made a good start against Len Greenery's Lola and Chris Ringrose's Ray; we appeared to break away from the gaggle behind, I was hounded by Greenery and Ringrose, managing to stave them off, taking the chequered flag, My first win in the John Player C.O.B. Time to celebrate. Martin, Ken, David, and Martins Boy's Jason and Nathon were ecstatic. Martins's ex-driver, Andy Best, attended. An extraordinary moment for Martin to have the GETEM GD 114 winning races. So far, we have won races in the Dunlop Autosport Star of Tomorrow Championship and now we have won in this year's C.O.B.Mega!!

Race 5. On the Grand Prix Circuit again, another win. With Kevin Gillen 2nd and Len Greenery 3rd. We seem to be on a roll.

Race 6. I spoke too soon, Ray's duo of Chris Creswell and Chris Ringrose got away, and Len Greenery and I were close behind in third and fourth. I was desperate to get a third win. I made a silly overtaking manoeuvre into Paddock that went wrong, causing me to spin out of contention. Thankfully the Getem was undamaged, apart from a barrow full of pebbles to get out of the car, which took forever. Teams are excellent, including the Getem Team. They get on with the job; apart from joking, they put up with us crazy drivers bringing back their beloved pristine cars.

Race 7 A last-lap thriller - After a couple of disappointing results, we need results, with the usual suspects at the sharp end of the grid, ie Greenery, Board, Ringrose, Creswell and myself; it looks like a tough call on paper. I was outside the front row and always made last-minute decisions on what to do. Instead of diving to the inside as we all tend to do on this occasion, I decided to drive around outside. The lights changed, and I made a tardy start, allowing the cars to charge up the inside. To begin with, they had the edge. But my decision proved to be the right one; I had loads of room. I was off the perfect entry line to Paddock, so I had to be careful; I needed to be alongside the leading bunch as we reached the mid-corner. My car seemed to lose traction, causing oversteer, ie the back lost grip. I managed to correct it; before the dip at the bottom of Paddock, I was ahead, managing to set myself up for Druids. From then on, I managed my lead, taking the chequered flag; for another win.

Race 8. It was, without doubt, the most memorable of 1984. It was a Sun Free Day, which attracted 30,000 spectators present. I claimed the pole with Ringrose and Chris Hall alongside me. Ringrose managed to get away first, with Hall and me close behind. Although very close, it remained status quo until the last lap; I was under Ringroses gearbox. As we exited Druids, I saw a backmarker spinning just before the entry to Graham Hill. Ringrose decided to get past the backmarker on the right; I decided to try the left to hope I would have the momentum to come out ahead as we exited Graham Hill. It didn't quite work out; we were side by side along the bottom bend; I knew this would be a game of nerves on who would give in—Ringrose wasn't, I wasn't. Ringrose wouldn't move an inch; I was almost on the grass. Our front wheels touched I could see smoke from the rubbing tyres. I stayed focused on the entry to Surtees; I've got the apex, Ringrose still with me, turning into Clearways. Ringrose runs out of room; he has to lift. I've got this race in the bag, just a couple hundred yards until I take the Chequered Flag, moving me back to second place in the Championship.

What a race. I will never forget what Brian Varney shouted when I got out of the car. What a driver!!. I love to see a happy Sponsor. The great Brian Jones always interviewed the top three drivers high up on top of Race control. I remember seeing 30-odd thousand spectators around the circuit. It was a fantastic spectacle; once interviewed, it was down to do a lap of honour, and this time Sponsor Brian Varney followed up in my race car, which was a special occasion for him, I bet. I've included the pic of the lap of honour with Brian following up behind, have a look a Chris Ringrose to my left; it's a look of disbelief that I won that race, and Chris Hall to my right; I bet he was hoping we may come together which would enable him to take a win. Chris Hall is a competitor, a bloody hard one too. In the next couple of years, we will be the two drivers competing to win in most races, so there is no time for pleasantries, eh Chris? However, we ended up best buddies when we stopped racing against each other and are still thirty-five years later. I call him Albi or Albert (after Albert Hall).

# CHAPTER 17

## BRIAN VARNEY

Major Sponsor Brian Varney of Legal Services was busy promoting and managing regular write-ups in the Newspapers. Brian managed to get us the entire window of the Building Society to promote our race programme; I would pop past it every day just to have a look, the display was on for a month!

Brian got his friend and fellow sponser Johnny Wier of Ashford Accident Repair Centre, to tow our Racecar around Ashford High in the Ashford Carnival, which was great fun. We had Martin, Ken, and David in team overalls, me in my race suit, and my wife Anne and our two girls in Red, all waving and handing out leaflets. It certainly gave awareness to the local Race Driver and Team. Brian was always on the case, generating new sponsors and promoting the Team, something I couldn't possibly have done to that extent. Brian was not only making sure we raced in '84 but looking ahead to 1985, which I left to him. I was so happy to enjoy the moment, I'm still pinching myself.

As well as the promotion mentioned, we managed to get sponsorship from Steve Brown of Sebron; who owned one of the top hospitality suits overlooking most of Brands Hatch Indy Circuit. It certainly proved a great way to entertain potential and existing sponsors. It was a bloody good job I decided from the offset to keep records of my racing in large folders container every race, qualifying and race, with pics and write-ups from Autosport Motoring News and local papers, which I put out for guests to read. I would pop up to meet the guests after practice and the race, with hopefully a smile on my face, and maybe a Garland around my neck. It was great getting a round of applause as you entered the Hospitality Suit. These folders have proven invaluable whilst writing this book; I don't think many drivers did anything like this. I soon realised that a sponsored driver must be approachable, not just good in their race car, something I worked hard on quickly became part and parcel of what a driver has to do if you want to hang on to your sponsors.

I even got sponsorship for a road car, a fab little car for Anne and a Fiat Turbo from Atlas Auto Hire Ashford, which I swapped every six months for a newer model. It was a three-year deal, Mega.

# CHAPTER 18

## BACK TO THE 1984 CHAMPION OF BRANDS

It's now late September. After that memorable win putting me back to second in the championship in front of thirty thousand spectators, the team is on a high.

Qualifying for round 8 on the Grand Prix Circuit: It was an oversubscribed race with drivers from abroad; they tend to book into a couple of Brands' races to help them prepare for the biggest formula Ford race of the year, the Formula Ford Festival in October. It attracted at least two hundred and fifty drivers going through heats, quarter finals & semi-finals to make the highly prestigious final. This meeting means everything to teams and drivers; back then, it was a massive stepping stone to catapult drivers into F3 and, hopefully, their journey to F1.

This race which I would love to win wasn't going to be easy, there were several hard chargers, including Damon Hill, the son of F1 World Champion Graham Hill. Damon had changed from a successful time racing bikes to single-seaters. Plus a few front runners from overseas. Over the moon, I qualified on Pole with the usual suspects behind with Damon Hill in 7th, which took the pressure off worrying about him.

The Race! I made a fabulous start, something I tend to do; I thank being a speedway rider for that, as it was imperative you got out of the gate in front. It was flat into the first corner; all my starts in ff1600 were the same, it gave me the edge most of the time. It was a war of nerves leading into Paddock. My GD114 was a handful; I ran wide at Clearways, Glen Board catching me down the main straight. I somehow managed to block Glen in his Ray, into Paddock. Ringrose took advantage of all this and moved up to second at Graham Hill bend but hit my wayward GETEM at Clearways. Ringrose spun immediately and badly hampered Board. I rotated a few yards up the road, causing confusion and collecting Hill in a fairly big way. Sorry, Damon. I was spitting feathers! I walked behind the pit land Garages, obviously still in race mode. I could see Judy Down, Martins's wife walking toward me; she came up and said, what went wrong? I was very childish, so I threw my helmet hard onto the concrete and shouted to her. What the F.....g Hell do you think went wrong? Within seconds a Marshall came over and said Rick, this is the second time we have seen you throwing your Helmet, the last time was at the bottom of Paddock, he said, sorry Rick, I have to do this; he cut the helmet straps off and stopped me from using it.

I had calmed down then and suddenly realised how I had treated poor Judy. I went straight to her and apologised unreservedly; I also told Martin how horrible I had been; he was ok and said he understood. I was so embarrassed; thankfully, it all blew over. Martin discovered it was a suspension failure, no wonder the GD114 was impossible to drive. That's motor racing, as they say.

# CHAPTER 19

## MY CRUEL BLOW

On the 22nd of October 1984, I was on my way to work with my trusty labourer Rob Wills; I called him Gums because he had lost two of his top teeth playing football, I believe. We were having our usual banter about all sorts of rubbish. I was applying Tyrolean to the outside of forty Council Houses near Folkestone, only a few miles down the road from where I lived in Sellindge. As I approached a very sharp right-hand corner, a Murphy's Road Contractor's Land Rover appeared on my side; he was head-on. I remember trying to swerve left to avoid it; the kerbing was very high, so my vehicle bounced back into the road; he caught the front driver's side of my Ford Escort Estate Car; the last thing I remember is a horrible thud; I then passed out. Whilst I lay unconscious in the car, Gums luckily found a house just yars away; he asked them to call the ambulance and Police. I was unconscious for quite a while, when I came around the first thing I did was call Gums over and say, have I been drinking? He just laughed and said, don't be so daft, it's only nine o'clock in the morning. I noticed the fire brigade was present; Gums kept me informed of what was happening. I was on Gas and Air, which helped the pain. The fire brigade had to take the driver's door and roof off; they planned to cut the back of my seat off and then slide me out through the back. It took two hours to cut me out of the car. I can't remember being taken to Ashford Hospital, about ten miles away, but I was in excruciating pain. I wasn't sure how serious this accident was. The doctor wasn't sure either, so it was off to X-ray to find out. My wife Anne got a call from the Hospital to explain that I was involved in an accident, and had been admitted to Ashford Hospital; Anne said she was ok to drive there, and they told her to be careful and take care. I was in A&E in a great deal of pain, when Anne arrived. The doctor informed me that my FEMA was a clean break; the ball joint at the top of my Fema had utterly separated. Also, my Pelvis had shattered in sixteen places, and to top it off, I was bleeding profusely from nasty facial cuts, the worst being a split above the top lip needing several stitches.

The Doctor explained the way forward. He will fit a Dynamic Condylar Screw used to join the Ball back to the FEMA by screwing into the Ball and attaching an eight-inch down bar to the FEMA by screws. The same bloody leg as the speedway accident, poor Anne, as if she hasn't had enough of her Hubby breaking bones.

I'm hoping for a speedy recovery but a little concerned; listening to the Doctor, it all sounds complicated; I hope the Dynamic Condylar Screw will do the job and screw it all together, fingers crossed. Because the accident was at eight o'clock in the morning, they could do the operation later that day. It just goes to show you never know what's around the corner. Excuse the pun. They got me ready for the operation and gave me the pre-med, so now just a wait for the Porters to take me down to the theatre. Waiting for the Porter seems to be forever; I'm thinking about all sorts of things, work and the championship; I have to say goodbye to that now, which is a bastard.

I recall going to the theatre, having the jab, and drifting away. Like everyone else that has an operation, the next thing we knew was coming around in the ward. I remember coming around. The nurses were plentiful and even had a Matron; back then. The nurse said she was going to look to see if all was ok; she looked and noticed my stomach was very swollen, which seemed to cause concern; the next thing I knew, a doctor arrived, who examined, pushed, and pressed me about; he worried I might have a damaged spleen. However, he asked the Matron to measure around my waist every hour, which didn't seem difficult. Would you believe they only had one tape measure, so every time they needed to measure me was a case of running around for that tape measure, then lifting me, which was bloody painful as they slid the tape under me?

To make it easy. I asked Brian Varney to bring a tape measure. I got Brian to slide the tape under my back, leaving the two ends of the tape jutting out; all they had to then was to lay the tape across my belly to get the measurement. The Nurse could now constantly check my swollen belly with relative ease, which didn't seem to be getting any smaller

On day two in the ward, I wasn't feeling well and began to feel sick. I pressed the alarm button to alert a Nurse; luckily, she grabbed a bowel as I brought up red stuff, which looked like blood. I was getting worried, knowing the Doctor was concerned about my spleen. My stomach reduced in size almost immediately; the doctor came, examined me and went away. The Doctor returned with a couple of students, asked if I minded them examining me; I didn't have a problem with that. The Doctor said "good news, Rick, thankfully, your Spleen is in good working order". My stomach was so swollen because the injuries to my face caused bleeding. When I went unconscious, I swallowed quite an amount of blood. Praise the Lord, hopefully recovery can begin in earnest

Cards! It wasn't just the odd one or two; I received over two hundred get-well-soon cards, which I've saved in a portfolio. I couldn't believe I was that popular; even Big John, the Paddock Marshall from Brands, sent me a card with a lovely letter.

Visitors, at times, there were fifteen around the bed. It was fantastic to see them all, but I have to say fantastic when they all went. I had Ashford Radio interview me and a couple of local newspapers popped in for an article, all down to sponsor Brian Varney.

It was much better being in a Hospital only three miles from home, unlike the trek for the family and sponsors to Hackney Hospital in London during my speedway days. I got on famously with Nurses and Matron, whom I nicknamed my little Strepsil, she said one day, "Mr Shortle, do you know what a strepsil is?" I remarked I hadn't got a clue; she said it was a bloody throat tablet, to which she laughed, so I continued calling her my little strepsil.

It's been a week now since the accident. I seem to be recovering well; when the surgeon visits the following Monday, I hope he will allow me to take my first steps. I continued to improve for the next couple of weeks; I was never without visitors, which helped the days pass quickly. Getem GD Racing Sponsors and Brian Varney of Legal Services hinted that he has some terrific news for me but will tell me all about it when I'm out of Hospital. Martin Down was full of ideas for 1985; he congratulated me on my performance at Brands and cannot wait to get out next year. This bloody accident curtailed my chance of winning the C.O.B. at my first attempt and pissed me off; however, the Team, Brian and all my sponsors were very happy with the results achieved so far and wished me a successful 1985.

Back to my recovery; it's Monday morning. I'm waiting to see the Surgeon. When he did arrive, I had everything crossed. With a bit of bending my leg and fiddling about with my pelvis, he was very pleased with my progress and will allow me to take a few steps without bearing weight on the broken leg. Before he left, he wanted to see me on crutches, little did he know I had over two sodding years been on crutches after my speedway accident, so crutches didn't bother me. I did the test, and that box ticked; I could use the loo, which meant not having to pea in a funny-shaped bottle. I was allowed to take a shower, freedom at last.

I was in Ashford William Harvey Hospital for twenty-three days; I didn't try to go home too soon as I did at Hackney after the Speedway accident. Not a good idea, and it wasn't fair to Anne. I had to stay in bed and let the broken pelvis heal; lucky for me, the pelvis is the fastest healing bone in your body.

# CHAPTER 20

## WAS THIS THE RIGHT DECISION?

I know a lot is going on behind the scenes; Martin has lots to tell me regarding the 1985 GETEM GD115, and Brian has news for me; roll on 1985, I knew that Brian Varney talked about works drives with leading ff1600 manufacturers Van Dieman, Reynard, Laser,and Ray. These manufacturers are the big players who turn out hundreds of formula Fords yearly. I had been beating them in a one-off car, Martin Downs Getem GD, giving me so much creditability, let alone winning against them.

Brian arranged for me to become works assisted driver for Reynard, run by Mike Parks, alongside Tim Jones, son of Legendary Brands Hatch Commentator Brian Jones and ex-owner of Brands Hatch Motor Racing stables. Heart-wrenching,but success brings decisions, some of which didn't rest comfortably with me. Now I had to carry out the most challenging thing since I told Brian Elmer I would no longer race speedway. I had to tell Martin Down that I can no longer drive his beloved GD GETEM CAR, which will be very upsetting.

Martin was due to arrive, I told Anne I had to tell Martin straight away. Letting him chatter about the plans for next year will be unfair, and I was bloody dreading it. At the time, I was still in bed, recovering. The doorbell rang; it was Martin; I told myself to stick to the plan, I could see Martin step into the entrance hall from my bedroom, we owned a bungalow. I welcomed him into the bedroom, he had his usual big smile, I didn't want to do this, but I had to. I burst out with something

71

like, "Martin; I don't know how to say this; I will not be racing for you next year"; there was total silence; I could see Martins's face, he looked devastated. He just said he didn't understand why! and tried to get me to change my mind. I explained that the decision wasn't just mine; I had a major sponsor in Brian Varney of Legal Services. Martin said "Get well soon" as he left, completely deflated. I felt a right bastard. I'm sure Martin feels proud to have produced a driver that's offered the chance to drive for Van Diemen and Reynard. He is hopefully happy with everything we did together, including winning many races in his GETEM GD chassis. I thank Martin and just thought, Ken, for so many fantastic memories. When testing for the 1985 Championship begins in a couple of months, all this will have blown over. Hopefully, Martin would have found a driver for his car; fingers crossed.

To this very day I look back with regret that Brian and I had made the decision to leave Getem GD Racing. Martin and I were like brothers, we both helped to move his wonderful Getem GD ff1600 forward. I rememember our conversations as if it was yesterday, including his desire to build his own F3 car, Martin felt my style would be good for F3 and was convinced he could produce a competitive car. When I look back, hindsight is a wonderful thing, I should have stayed. I believe Brian and myself were green horns in the racing world, we never realised how brilliant Martn Down was. I suppose we both thought these manufactors with big transporters and works drivers was the way to go but we very soon found out to our cost it wasn't.

# CHAPTER 21

## THE RAC NATIONAL FF1600 CHAMPIONSHIP

I had a couple of months to prepare myself for testing. At the moment, I'm far from being fit, and to top that, the surgeon has advised me not to race until I have the metal removed in eighteen months. An accident may damage it even further if the metal is still in the leg. I decided to race with the metal. I managed to put the sadness of leaving Martin Down behind me, focusing on the new and hopefully exciting challenge ahead.

Probably the biggest challenge of my short motor racing career. I was a work-assisted driver for one of the best manufacturers of Formula Ford 1600. Reynard Racing Cars. Based on their success in 1984, we both felt and were hoping the all-new 1985 would follow the success of the 84. Brian took me to the Reynard Factory; even the look of the exterior blew my mind, nothing like the beloved Getem Factory, a garage at the top of the garden. The man in charge, Rick Gorne, gave us a tour of the factory; it was terrific, that alone did the selling job; Brian loves that sort of thing; I agree from a sponsor's point of view; it's bloody impressive.

Brian made a deal for me to become a work-assisted Reynard driver. We visited the team running Tim Jones and myself in the 1985 RAC ff1600 Championship. Mike Parkes was a Brummie, an ex-ff1600 racer turned Team owner, he ran Tim Jones in the previous year's championship in an 84 Reynard, so everything seemed good. He ran his Race Team from the rear of his Tyre fitting business near Birmingham. I let Brian talk; he

73

was very professional, always dotted the eyes, and crossed the T's. Brian seemed to get on ok with Mike Parkes. All the paperwork was sorted out and I'm now a fully signed up Reynard 1985 ff1600 Assisted Works Driver. The first test day is Silverstone, date to be advised. I can't wait.

In between times, Brian organised the launches of the 1985 Reynard ff1600. First, in Sellindge Village Hall, we put the car on display and invited existing and potential sponsors. I made a speech thanking everyone, promising to give 100%. Next, a press release at Brians's new home in Willesborough, Ashford Kent, attended by the Lady Mayor of Ashford, local press, etc., and then on to the garage Brian used in Wye where the Reynard was on display in their Showrooms for a few days followed by a cheese and wine party. Things certainly feel more professional; I'm ready to get back in a race car to see what I can do after my nasty accident.

Silverstone & Cadwell. At last, we have a date for testing Silverstone and Cadwell. Still limping somewhat, I've declared myself fit enough to race. Silverstone was to shake the car down and get an idea of what we all thought of the car, it certainly looked like the business, but will it be the business? My first drive in what I felt should be night and day better than the "Getem" was dissapointing, it was unstable, and the front end would dart about under braking; not enjoyable at all to drive, not impressed, but as it was the first test we had to give time to carry out some development, however, nothing Mike Parks Racing did made any difference. We were lucky to get into the top ten lap times by the end of the day. I always kept Brian Varney up to speed; we agreed to give it another test day and do the first race to get an idea of where we were.

The next test was two days at Cadwell Park, which didn't improve; I had an off, causing damage to the driving side suspension, and we needed to replace a wishbone, but the team didn't carry any spares. If I wanted to get out the next day, it meant driving to Reynard in Bicester to collect the spares, some hundred and fifty miles, then the same back to Cadwell, which I did with my wife, Anne. Brian was livid; about me going to Bicester. The test the next day didn't make any remarkable difference. At the moment, I didn't feel like the same old Rick of last year; the only pleasing thing was that my lap times weren't far away from teammate Tim Jones. Last year most of the time, I was the quickest in the Getem GD Car.

Race one - Silverstone. We qualified sixth and ninth, respectively, and apart from the usual frantic start that's ever-present in ff1600, Tim and I had reasonably lonely races. However, at least we slightly improved our lap times, but still not quick enough, and finally, we brought both cars home.

Race two - Oulton Park. Although I managed to qualify twelfth, the race for Tim Jones and myself was a nightmare; we were sidelined with more problems. Another disappointing day.

I felt sorry for sponsor Brian Varney, who wasn't a happy Teddy. I couldn't go home with Brian as he drove up separately; I had teammate Tim Jones as a company. On the way home, I didn't say much to Tim about the problems we were both having; as Brian was my Manager, I felt it was best if he spoke to Mike Parks. I was fucking hating this supposedly great move forward; it was nothing like I expected. I wonder if we have made one hell of a mistake leaving Martin Down, we couldn't go back if we tried. Martin has another driver, a Canadian by the name of Rob Murphy.

# CHAPTER 22

## WELCOME, ROB CRESSWELL RACING SERVICES

The next day I went to see Brian to discuss the way forward.

We both agreed that the Reynard ff1600 1985 was an uncompetitive car. The best way forward was to approach another team with an available competitive car. I suggested we talk to Rob Cresswell Racing Services. Rob Cresswell is a red-hot engineer; they have run two ff1600 in the Champion of Brands for the last five years, producing three Champions; they also ran Allard Karllf in the Benelux ff2000 Championship abroad, winning that Championship too. Just as importantly, we have raced against them at Brands over the last couple of years, so we know each other; they are a great team with no airs or graces. Brian approached them and struck a deal, only a bit different from what we were thinking; Rob had a couple of Reynards 84's, not ff1600 but ff2000, which looked like real race cars with wings and slick tyres. The best looking ff2000 ever made. The deal was to run me in a few races in 1985, including the highly prestigious BBC Grandstand winter series at the end of the year and see how it goes, and then decide about doing a full ff2000 Championship in 1986, or returning to ff1600 instead. We both felt it was a good idea; I left Brian to do the paperwork, we had a few weeks to wait, so Brian, not one to stand still, booked me a test in the works ff1600 Van Dieman and a test in a Reynard ff2000 just to see how I got on.

My first ff2000 race was on March 30/31st at Brands Hatch, which is fantastic news as I know Brands well. Even better, I have a day of testing

77

before the race. I went along to Rob Cresswell Racing for a seat fitting. It was a great big wow seeing the ff2000 race car with wings and slicks; it looks different from the ff1600. I can't wait to drive it. Having raced against the Rob Cresswell Racing Drivers Chris Cresswell and Chris Ringrose, two rapid drivers, I had battled for wins over the last couple of years. I was aware it was a good team with an excellent track record, and they also knew my track record; all this knowledge helped break the ice very quickly.

Their workshop was immaculate. The two ff2000 Reynards sitting side by side looked terrific—one for Allard Kalff, who is doing the Benelux ff2000 Championship, which he won. The other is for little me. It's incredible how one soon forgets the crap moments; most of us drivers seem to forget the past, dust ourselves off and look forward to the next chapter. Having spent the day with Rob and his right-hand man, pipe smoking Dave Linstead, I found it enjoyable and very much like being back with Martin Down. Somehow; I had a feeling my time with RCR was going to be a great one. I left Rob and Dave in high spirits, and I can declare the old Rick is back. Thanks Brian.

# CHAPTER 23

## A TASTE OF FF2000

I only have a few days to wait until testing, which I'm looking forward to; it will be interesting to see how Rob compares with Mike Parks and Martin Down; I bet you've all noticed I keep mentioning Martin Down. I can't help it because I use him as the benchmark; I'm still on cloud nine, a race driver.

Test day at Brands Hatch. I got Brother Dave with me today; he's not been for a while, and sadly not so good these days, but he's a fighter and will attend as much as he can; I'm so pleased he's there today watching and putting his in two pennyworth Rob booked a Pit lane garage, and the car looks impressive, first thumbs up from Bro. Dave Linstead is already making a welcome to the Team cuppa, which we sup during a rundown from Rob, who is a very quiet talker but very professional. I feel pretty special being part of this team. I can't wait to slide into the cockpit; and now I seem to be shaking with hopeful excitement. We had a couple of visitors in our Garage before testing began, including Marcus Pye of AutoSport and Ace ff1600 ff2000 driver, John Pratt.

At last, it's time, and the klaxon has sounded. Out I go to join the other cars, ready to test. Brands always give me more buzz as I leave the pits to go onto the track than any other Circuit. Thankfully, the weather is good for my first-ever run in the Reynard ff2000. It felt much better than I envisaged it would have been; I'm nowhere near what the car can do but I feel confident we will improve during the day. I did a few laps to get the

In-Pit Board, so in I came. I had a chat with Rob, who gave me some advice on how to get a bit more out of the car; amazingly, it worked and my lap times came tumbling down. The day was all about doing more of the same.

Rob was a perfectionist.; I would sit in the car for what seemed hours whilst he made minor adjustments; if he checked them once, he would check them a hundred times. Rob was infuriating, but what I can say is that I may do fewer laps testing, but you could guarantee they would be fantastic laps.

Luckily there were quite a few ff2000 drivers out there, enabling us to get an idea of where we were; I was ninth quickest out of twenty drivers, with quite a few big names present, with Dave Coyne, John Pratt, Ross Hockenhull, and Johnathan Bancroft, to name but a few. My lap times were impressive for the first test, so all in all, a good day. Rob was pleased with the progress. Qualifying. Sadly I had an electrical problem and only managed to make seventeenth on the grid. And now for the Race. My first ff2000 race ever was daunting, and even more so with me being back in seventeenth. To cut a long story short, I had a great race and finished in seventh place, happy with that and so were the Team. oll on to the next Race, this time at Silverstone.

Brian Varney informed Reynard why we had withdrawn from the works-assisted drive. He struck a deal to which allowed him to change back to an 84 ff1600 Reynard (it was teammate Tim Jones's car). We knew it was a fantastic car. We took delivery of the vehicle and handed it over to Rob Cresswell to keep it in ff1600 guise. I'm so pleased Brian is in the Legal profession, it must be an advantage in this sort of situation

The next race was at Silverstone. After a reasonable first race at Brands, we were upbeat for our next outing on the Silverstone Grand Prix Circuit. Qualifying, I was only marginally slower than the four fastest drivers; we were ecstatic, and I made the third row of the grid. And now the race, I made a good start, which is typical for me. I was up in third place before completing the first lap. I had to be realistic, as the two drivers ahead were far more experienced than me; I could see them slowly pulling away; I decided to make sure I kept my third place safe; I was buzzing under my helmet; I didn't expect to be in third place in my second race in an ff2000. After a few laps, I could tell I wasn't under pressure from the drivers behind and I managed to maintain my position in third past the chequered flag. Team -Sponsor Brian Varney, David and I were delighted with the result.

# CHAPTER 24

## BACK TO FF1600 AND FF2000

I wasn't quite sure of the plan of attack for the rest of this season; that's obviously up to Brian. Will it be more of ff 2000 or back to ff1600? But this time, I'm in a Reynard, not Martin Downs's beloved Getem GD car, which will be interesting. Brian called me and explained I would be racing in the Reynard ff1600 at Brands Hatch on the Brands Sun Free Day, which is excellent news. It is a big meeting with crowds of over 30,000. I will return to my old hunting ground, racing against the usual suspects plus some new ones. I will test in a week with a race the following weekend.

I have already raced the Reynard in 2000 guise; now that is has been converted to 1600, I hope it doesn't feel too different. I will find out when I test in a week—I can't wait. On testing day David was fit enough to come along. He's not so critical of late, and that's either down to my performances or just that he's suffering health-wise. I would rather it wasn't his health; he never complains about that. I had a surprise visitor, none other than the rapid ff1600 driver John Pratt. Rob knew him well, more so than me; he came along to see if he could help and advise; John raced an 84 Reynard to great success last year.

Time to give it a run. Usual first time out for temperature checks etc., in after five laps to tell Rob what I thought; it felt terrific. We will learn more after trying to get the best out of it. Lap times were dropping nicely. I seem to knock a little time off each time I go out; I'm now complaining of understeer, luckily John Pratt is still with us and suggests to Rob what to try. Luckily Rob happened to have the parts available in his van.

I jumped out of the Reynard and had a cuppa whilst Rob and Pipe smoker Dave, fit the parts required. As mentioned before, Rob is a perfectionist; I, therefore, expected the fitting to take a while. It gave me time to chat with JP, which I found interesting, as did my Bro taking his usual stance on his shooting stick. It made me feel great chatting talking to JP. The parts have now been fitted and out we go; let's see how we get on. I did five laps and came in; the car felt quite different; Rob would watch me going through corners; he could tell what the car was doing. I pitted and chatted with Rob; he adjusted the front end, and I went out again. This time it felt even better; I had just knocked half a second of what was already a good time, and I was the quickest ff1600 out there (Mega Wowzer).

I loved testing more than the race; it's incredible how engineers can squeeze more out of the car as long as the driver is doing his bit behind the wheel. Sponsor / Manager Brian Varney arrived late morning; he was more than impressed with the progress, which makes me happy; we don't want a miserable sponsor/manager, do we? It was a fabulous day of testing; the car, Team and driver performed well. We are very much looking forward to the race next week—the Champion of Brands ff1600 -Sun Free Day Meeting.

As usual in motorsport, everybody has crap days and good days; it looks as if we are returning to the good days after racing or trying to race the most uncompetitive Reynard 1985. It's such a boost when everything is going well; believe me, you tend to doubt yourself. I'm looking forward to getting back in 1600 and hopefully getting a good result for us all.

Qualifying on Saturday. It was good to be back to the old stamping ground—still, lots of regular front runners in the list of competitors. On paper, Colin Stancombe is the man to beat. All assembled, ready to drive through the tunnel; I must get my head down from the word go; in the past, when I qualified Martin Downs Getem, on most occasions, I got my fastest lap on the third lap, nine times out of ten it was quick enough to get pole.

The whistle blows to start qualifying, out we go. I was third in line to get out, I preferred to be first but Stancombe is, I need to get past him

ASAP; I'm now chasing after Stancombe, I do my best but can only qualify second, disappointing but not the end of the world.

The Race. The Sun Free Day Champion of Brands ff1600. I won this race last year. Can I do the double? This meeting attracts over 30,000 spectators; it is a magnificent spectacle, The Brands Hatch Indi Circuit, being bowel-like, viewing from ninety per cent of wherever you are will allow you to see most of the entire circuit; there's nothing like it anywhere. I can't wait to get on the grid. On the grid Stancombe is on pole, I'm middle of the front row; the green flag waved for the warm-up lap. As we dip into Paddock Hill Bend, I follow Colin into the corner, tight on the painted kerbs; I notice how dry and dusty the ground is the other side of the kerbs. If Colin Stancombe beat me off the line, I would duck in behind him as we dived into Paddock Hill Bend; providing there is room, I would put my outside wheels on the dusty stuff on the other side of the kerbing and go for it. Back on the grid, all stationary, it seemed ages before the lights changed, five-second board and were off, sod it didn't make a googd start, quickly back to plan "B", dive to my right to get behind Stancombe.

Paddock flat out in third! Ok, Ricky Boy, do your worst; Colin will be livid. We arrive at Paddock; Stancombe leaves me enough room to keep my inside wheels on the actual track; I place my car straddling the kerbs; now it's just a matter of keeping my foot in, hopefully coming out the other side in front of Stancombe. It's bloody bumpy and uncomfortable, dust everywhere; I'm back on the circuit before Colin catches me; I need to keep a tight line up to the hairpin Druids. Hopefully, I can settle down, pace myself, and win this race in front of thirty-odd thousand people. The race settled down. I kept a little distance between myself and Stancombe, taking the chequered flag for a win and fastest lap. Now for the fireworks-Mr Stancombe was furious. He was having a right go at me from the time I got out of the car; he gave me an earful up to the presentation tower saying it was out of order, etc. I felt the best thing to do was to keep quiet. Brian Jones interviewed me, welcoming me back to winning; they didn't mention the first lap incident; apart from that was an awe-inspiring start, Rick; I replied it was the safest thing to do as I didn't want to apply my brakes or hit Colin up the rear, Colin was still seething!

Brian Varney, Rob, Pipe smoking Dave and Bro were over the moon; it was back to the pits to celebrate, which fell flat when Mr Stamcombe arrived at our setup in the competitors parking area. He was still fuming, then informed me he had launched a complaint with the clerk of the course, which has been upheld. Therefore the race win has been taken away; I should hand him the winner's trophy and garland. I remarked to Colin that I had won that race and pushed the cup into his chest; as I stated, you can have the Trophy but not the winner's Garland. Dave, the Pipe Lindsey, felt it would be no use trying to dispute the result; we all know we won it fair and square; this is Formula Ford, not bloody Tiddley Winks. As we were packing away, many spectators congratulated me and felt it was tough taking the win away. Brian Varney was in good spirits. He even put a quarter page in Autosport congratulating his driver Rick Shortle and Rob Cresswell Racing Services for winning on the road. What a fabulous weekend; I'm so upbeat. My mojo is back. The team is superb; I wonder what the rest of 1985 will bring.

Let's do another ff2000. At least once a week, Anne and I pop around to Brian and Judy's for a few glasses of wine and a chat. We discuss the racing and how things are going; Early 1985 was disappointing due to a uncompetative Reynard. Having said that, it's turning out to be an exciting 85; I'm enjoying every minute of it, even though Martin Down is still on my mind. I'm getting to know and understand Rob Cresswell and Dave the Pipe Linstead; I feel just as settled as I did with Martin Down.

I digress. Brian was very upbeat and suggested I squeeze in another ff2000 race, more for practice than anything else, as he would like me to contest the prestigious BBC Grandstand ff2000 Championship which is in early December, shortly after the ff1600 Festival. Wow, what a schedule – I'm going to be so busy. These races will be tough, they will include well-known, established drivers, and a few that will go on to race Formula One. My Top Ten for the BBC Grandstand Championship, in no particular order are, Martin Donelly, Eddie Irvine, Gary Brabham, Benoit Vigneault, John Pratt, Julian Bailey, Ross Hockenhull, Dave Coyne, Mark Blundell, and Neil Cunningham plus many more in a probable field of 28. Many of these drivers have entered the BBC Grandstand Championship in previous years. I'm going to need my big boy pants on for this one. I was buzzing. I love racing the Reynard 2000; Rob Cresswell recons it suits my smooth driving style; we shall see.

Brian Varney has sorted the next ff2000 race in ten days; it should give us a good idea of how I fair against all these Aces. I was looking forward to showing promise in this warm-up race that will put me in good stead for the BBC Grandstand Championship, run a few weeks after the Formula Ford Festival, which is run during the last week in October.

When qualifying for the ff2000, there was unfortunately an electrical problem with the car; whatever Rob and Dave the Pipe did to cure it was to no avail. I qualified seventeenth out of twenty-six drivers, so I had a lot to do in this race. After qualifying, Rob and Dave managed to find the route of the problem which meant we had a fast car for the race.

In spite of all our problems, we all kept smiling. Brian was ok and now realises things can go wrong that are out of the team's control for a short time. Because Rob Cresswell Racing Services are a polished, sound setup, they managed to get the car back to its full potential. It's now down to the driver to work his way through the field. Working my way up from seventeen will not be easy, I have no delusions of grandeur here.

The Race. I'm outside on the eighth row, a long way back for a twenty-lap race. I have completed the warm-up lap. I made my plan of attack: to try to beat the guy in sixteenth place off the line. I made a blinding start and a right-hand diagonal line aiming to be ahead ASAP, which was successful. By the time we roared across the start-finish line and then headed towards Paddock Hill Bend, all the cars were bunched together. As we all dropped down Paddock Hill, I was hoping one or two in front of me would run wide, allowing me to make a place or two; a couple did go wide, and I had momentum as we all began to rise towards Druids, you do have to have your wits about you on the opening lap here. I think I made three places before Druids Hairpin; I need to keep pushing as it will get more challenging once the race settles down. I manage to nip up inside another driver into Clearways. Thankfully he left enough room for me to get through. The bunch ahead got away but was catchable. So

I got my head down and focussed on reeling them in. I could tell I was getting nearer. It took three of four laps to be within striking distance; I was now up with the quick drivers; Julian Baily was next, and I followed him for a couple of laps. I felt better than him through Paddock, but not by much. I decided to make my move on the next lap, and the only way was to come alongside him as we approached the entry to Paddock, hoping Julian would hold a tight line as we dipped into Paddock. I could then tiptoe around the outside with the hope of nudging in front as we rise to Druids. So here I go, committed now, let's do this; the trouble with these ideas is that they always seem easy. And when they go wrong like this is about to, you realise the speed you're going as you smash through the useless catch fencing they used back in the day, and bloody dangerous they were too. Baily and I touch we both go off together. Jesus, this felt quick; we both reached a standstill buried in the catch fencing and gravel.

While struggling to get out of my destroyed Reynard, I could see Julian walking towards me out of his car. By his body language alone, I can tell he's livid. To this very day, I remember that he put one hand on my steering wheel, ripped my visor off, then drew back his arm and punched me in the face; I was so lucky to end up with nothing worse than a nosebleed. I reckon it was a fifty/fifty shunt! Well, we would all say that, wouldn't we? But truthfully, it was an optimistic manoeuvre on my part.

Now back to the team to explain, How their pristine race car is now a wreck. Surprisingly they were all upbeat. Brian, who foots the bill, was disappointed but over the moon with my competitiveness—working my way up the field from way back in seventeenth place. Thank Christ for that, I tried my best, but I ran out of talent on this occasion. Brian never tells me the cost of anything; he's taken all that worry away. I suppose he wants me to focus on the racing. I didn't have a pot to piss in three seasons ago, all by chance. I've got what I have now—still living the dream.

The Formula Ford Festival is not far away, so it's back in an ff1600, followed by the BBC FF2000 Grandstand Championship a few weeks later.

# CHAPTER 25

## 1985 FF1600 FESTIVAL

The Formula Ford Festival in the eighties attracted around two hundred and eighty-plus drivers worldwide. Who was vying to make the final and, hopefully, the win?

By chance, I was at Brands in August 2019 and bumped into the Voice of Brands, "Brian Jones", outside the Brands Hatch Restaurant. We chatted! Mainly motor racing, which certainly included ff1600. Brians's enthusiasm for this formula and the Formula Ford Festival at his beloved Brand Hatch took over the conversation. Brian remembered my time in ff1600 and remarked the 1980s was, without doubt, the most competitive time for the Formula. It was a shock to hear that Brian died on New Years' Day 2021 at the age of 85; I am so pleased I managed to bump into him for that chat; he was a charming, delightful man gone but never forgotten. More of Brian later in my section about becoming a race instructor and earning a living within the motor racing Industry

FF1600 was a recognised platform to move up to Formula Three then Formula Two, hopefully, Form One. I never made these dizzy heights, but I am so pleased I was racing during the best years of Formula Ford. Sadly, in the nineties, many new Formulas were introduced, such as Formula Renault-Audi-BMW etc. This decision immediately gave drivers and teams too many choices, with budgets soaring through the roof. Only the well-heeled could move forward. So! unless one had a mega-budget, or you were cheeky chappies like Perry McCarthy, who worked miracles raising budgets, for which I applaud. Others, such as Johnny Herbert, got through with sheer talent and the help of ff1600 Quest owner Mike Thomson.

The Formula Ford Festival is a three-day event. Qualifying on Friday, Heats and Quarterfinals on Saturday, Semi-finals and the Grand Final on Sunday. Because it was a worldwide event, teams started to trickle in as early as the Monday before the event. General Practice for the event was available on Wednesday and Thursday.

Back then, the entire week was a fantastic great atmosphere. The paddock packed to the gunnels with Formula Fords, Big Teams, Small Teams and several with just a driver and helper. Brilliant. An exhibition dome is situated on the left just after you've entered the circuit. This particular show is like a mini motor show with all the current Formula Ford 1600 Manufactures including Van Dieman, Reynard, Ray, Swift, Quest, Lazer, Jamun to name but a few plus a couple of obscures such as the OX, Getem and Prowess, which was a fully enclosed example. Also on display were the engine builders. The Formula Ford 1600 engine is the old Kent engine and will require a rebuild every eight hours, doesn't seem much, but vital to keep the engine in top performance. Minister, Scholar, Auriga and Nelson were the engine tuners back then.

Duckham oils, sponsors of the Van Dieman Team had a stand, as did many others. It was a fantastic show, with a superb atmosphere attracting teams, drivers and spectators. Throughout the event, Ford Motor Company had a stand-in the Paddock where tea, coffee, soft drinks, and cakes were available, an excellent spot for drivers and teams to get together. Sadly the Festival is a shadow of its former self, but it's still a fab one.

The 1985 festival was the first festival I competed in with another team, Rob Cresswell Racing Services. They are an exceptionally well-put-together team, and I'm incredibly excited about this weekend's festival. If I drive well, focus, and things go my way, I believe I will end up on the podium. For whatever reason, I was relaxed and somehow felt different to the way I usually feel.

Like most of the other competitors, we were testing Wednesday and Thursday. I was looking forward to getting out on the track to see how well I would do against all these drivers from every corner of the world. The list of competitors was terrific. Damon Hill, Johnny Herbert, Mark Blundell, Peter Rogers, Tim Jones, Chris Hall, Rick Morris, Bertrand Cachot, Jonathan Bancroft, Allan Seedhouse, the Brazillian Paulo Carcasci plus many others. The atmosphere was electric; I was nervous but excited, all at the same time, itching to get out on the track. Rob Cresswell is calm and never looks flustered, which gives me confidence. We had the luxury of the Pit Lane garages with the ff2000 and Rob Cresswell Racing ran Dutchman Alard Karlf in the ff2000; not only that, our garage was the first one. Number one. Result. Being in the pit lane garages was a good bonus for all sorts of reasons; it would allow us to get in front of the queue for our qualifying, giving us an easier chance of a good lap time.

My time has now arrived. I'm about to qualify for the most crucial race in my ff1600 racing. I can feel slight tension between Rob Cresswell and pipe-smoking Dave Lynsted. It's exciting times. I want to do well, and do you know what? I'm really up for this; I am more excited than concerned, bring it on. My wife Anne and our two girls Tina and Julia are there, as is Brother David resting on his shooting stick, looking pleased. Sponsor Brian Varney and his wife Judy are there to support me. Thankfully, the Marshalls allowed more people in the garages and along the Pit wall, which wouldn't be the case today.

Dave is our spotter, looking for the cars in our qualifying session and making their way down towards us. I'm in the garage in my Reynard, all belted up and ready; the moment Dave gives us the signal, I get out ahead of the queue. It worked like a dream; I'm in front of twenty-seven formula fords, one or two disgruntled faces wondering how I got there. So this is it, just waiting for the Marshall to wave the green flag. I usually get on the throttle as soon as I get onto the circuit; it gets me in the zone. I'm hitting Paddock flat in third, then up towards Druids, down to second, working the tyres to get some heat into them as I negotiate Druids; I exit the corner. My beautiful Reynard feels ready. Next, Graham Hill Bend is a downhill, fast-sweeping corner. It was much more enjoyable before the circuit was increased in length to enable them to run Super Bikes, and it was ruining this wonderful part of the circuit.

I feel good; the car feels good—time to get the laps together. Just a quick look in the mirrors to see who's behind me, it's Damon Hill; he's not close, so it's head down and go for it. We get fifteen minutes of qualifying, which is ample as long as backmarkers do not hamper you, I tended to focus on a quick driver ahead and try to make ground on them, and it works for me. My Pit board altered from first to second quickest, and I was happy with that; the marshall hung the chequered flag to signal the end of qualifying for us. I ease off the throttle, gently do a slowing down lap, trickle down the pit lane, and start looking for pipe-smoking Dave, who will usher me into our garage; I see smiling faces; from Rob Cresswell and the team; that's a good sign.

Dave nips off for the qualifying sheet to see if the Teams lap times are correct; I've never known them not to be; however, it's always great to see them in black and white. I extrude myself from my beloved Reynard 84, wriggle out of the top part of my overalls, and pat the team on the back for giving me a fast car. Allard Karlf hugs me and congratulates me on doing a good job.

I still think of the Getem team, particularly Martin Down, and wonder how their driver Rob Murphy is getting on. Rob is going great guns, and why shouldn't he? The Getem is a brilliant car. I digress; I like writing what I am thinking, and at that moment in time, as I was writing about qualifying, I thought about my times with Getem Racing, which was very special. Now, where was I? Oh yes, waiting for confirmation of how well I qualified. I was second to Damon Hill, with my hero Rick Morris in the front row. Out Qualifying, my hero Rick Morris made my day; I knew it would be a tough race with Rick Morris alongside me in the front row. As I said earlier, I was in a good mindset and looking forward to my first race in the 1985 ff1600 Festival, earning a place in the front row. Next to Damon Hill, I was buzzing. Rob and pipe-smoking Dave were straight back checking the Reynard over; believe me, Rob will repeatedly check every nut and bolt until he's delighted he is 100 per cent happy.

Brother David is chuffed; I could tell by his demeanour, which made me happy; seeing my Bruv in such a good place even though he's full of pain is brilliant.

Heat One of the 1985 ff1600 Festival. Saturday morning, we were first out. Thankfully the track was dry, which was a stroke of luck; the Festival is always at the end of October, so it's typical to experience a damp circuit in the morning. I'm already in my race overalls, checking I have all my kit and my visor is clear; the sun, if there is any, is low in the sky this time of year, mainly through the Esses and as you turn into Clearways. I attach a strip of tape across my visor, leaving just an inch gap to see through. It looks drastic, but it works for me. So there we are, car ready, me ready, the race is in an hour; I try to relax. Back in 1985, a portacabin positioned perfectly along the bottom bend next to the slip road gets you back to the Paddock in an emergency. By chance, attached to the portacabin was a ladder, not much of one that gave you access to the roof, don't ask me how but with the team and help from Damon Hills Team, who wanted to get the best view of the Graham Hill bend as well, we managed to get Bro up there. Thank Teams. Across the tannoy address system, it's time for our race; they are always early, so there is no rush. I let the team decide, they know when. My thoughts aren't anything special I tend to go quiet and don't want to communicate with anyone, so the chirpy cheeky chappie, as I usually am, has somewhat gone into hiding. We are all different.

Front row Pole Damon Hill middle front row Shortle and on my left my hero Rick Morris. They say that pole at Brands is tricky because you enter Paddock on a tight line. The lights go green; Hill makes a cracking start; I tuck in behind him; Rick Morris's start is tardy, allowing Mark Peters to grab third. I am experiencing ff1600 at the top flight. Thankfully I'm not phased; it's bloody close. It was a close quartet through Paddock into and out of Druids, all flat through Graham Hill, all looking for a mistake by the other drivers but no mistakes made. I managed to hold my second position, Mark Peters did all he could to get past. However, my knowledge of Brands was invaluable, without a doubt, my most enjoyable race in an ff1600 to date. I finished second and got the fastest lap. Whilst racing, I got the odd glimse of my wife Anne, daughters Tina and Julia with Bro, sponsor Brian and and his wife Judy Varney, who were on top of the Portacabin alongside some of Damon Hills Team. After the race, Marshalls directed us into scrutineering and then back to the Team garage for a chat. We were all happy, I would have loved a win, but it wasn't to be. So second place it is, which puts me into the quarter finals. That's it for today. I have made the quarter final, hopefully I will make the semi final and then the Grand Final on Sunday; I can't wait.

And now for the quarter finals. Fast Peter Rogers on Pole is an exciting front row, with Damon Hill sitting snuggly between Rogers and John Butcher Booth outside on the front row. I felt comfortable sitting behind pole Man Peter Rogers on row two. My plan, if it works, is to follow Fast Pete into Paddock, then hopefully up the hill towards Druids holding station in the hope it will be clearer where I go from there after Druids is behind us. All went to plan, except Hill dived under Rogers into Paddock; I managed to get third, and Booth was close behind. Peter Rogers had the nose cone of the Lazer almost underneath Hill's gearbox. He was close, looking like an accident was about to happen; this continued for a couple more laps until Damon made a mistake. He ran wide before the apex at Paddock; Rogers went for it and got past Hill cleanly. It's fab, I had a front-row seat watching all of this. Because Damon ran wide, I felt I had a slight chance of getting past him; I followed Damon up the hill towards Druids Bend. He was not quite a car's width from the inside kerbing; I made a split-second decision and put my inside front wheels onto the grass, which was dry. I just about managed to stay away from his Van Diemen and come out in front as we exited Druids. I'm now up to second but know I will have a fight on my hands, keeping Hill behind me.

Even though we had battles Royal, we seemed to have pulled away from the pack behind. I was okay, in second place and trying to keep my head down. We're now on lap 7 of 15 I did a Damon Hill and ran wide, exiting Paddock. This time; it was advantage Hill; I could sense he was ready to pounce, and pounce he did in the dip at the bottom of Paddock; I had two options, one to block with a chance of taking us both out or hope he doesn't squeeze through, which he did, Bugger I was not happy. The remaining laps were status quo; Fast Peter had pulled out a gap between Hill and myself. I delighted that I had no problem staying with these young guns. Rogers took the chequered flag from Damon in second and me in third, not so far behind. So it will be the third row for me for the semi-final. If I didn't make that mistake at Paddock and let Damon through, I might have finished second.

Back to the garage for a cup of Pipe Smoking Daves tea, and a team chat. All in all, Rob Cresswell Racing Services are doing a fabulous job; the Reynard is a brilliant car to drive, and I'm enjoying every minute of this weekend. We are all looking forward to the semi-final and a place in the grand final, fingers crossed.

The semi-final. Yes, it's row three for me; I'm in the area where things happen, particularly on the opening lap. I have no plan of attack; try to be tidy, quick and trouble-free; yes, I know that is easier said than done. It's time for the semi-final. I'm a little nervous, still annoyed with myself for letting Hill through. Warm-up lap completed, back on the grid to wait for the green light, start-finish Marshall waves the 1 minute followed by the thirty-second board etc. Red lights are on, and all you hear are the engines revving. Greenlight, we go. It's a lottery as we dip into Paddock. I feel good, no dramas. Climbing the hill to Druids, I leave space in front in case someone has a moment. Sadly I did this all in vain as Mr Butcher Booth flew into the back of my beloved Reynard, launching me into cars, which had the concenteener effect; cars were flying everywhere. I parked outside Druids, my right front suspension still connected with the wheel at a funny angle. I managed to drive back to our garage, to get it fixed as the race was stopped whilst our lovely hard-working marshalls cleared up the mess at Druids; it looked like a breakers yard. As I was approaching our garage, I could hear the dulcet tones of Brian Jones, the voice of Brands, remarking he could see Shortle limping down the pit lane in his Reynard that was looking in a bad state of repair. Sadly Brian Jones was spot on; the front driver's side wishbones are beyond repair. Unfortunately, this is the end of the 1985 ff1600 Festival for me; we were all gutted.

On reflection, I felt Rob Cresswell, Dave Linstead and I did a pretty good job. After this Festival, I knew I could race against the best I could keep up with and beat the best Formula Ford 1600cc drivers from anywhere. Brian Varney, my sponsor, was disappointed, but he knows that in close racing like this, anything can happen and it did. My dear Bro David was hoping for more but knew I gave one hundred per cent. We had to dust ourselves off, pick ourselves up, and start again.

I was still buzzing and feeling very good about myself; I felt much more confident about my driving and knew I would be a better driver with my experience over this Festival.

The 1985 Formula Ford Festival was fantastic; a confident Johnny Herbert won the final, Jonathan Bancroft runner up with Damon Hill third. Unfortunately, Peter Rogers, my favourite to win, had an off and finished a lowly thirteenth.; If only Butcher Booth didn't decide to run into the back of my Reynard it could have been me in that final, who knows what the outcome might have been? Although 1985 started badly with an uncompetitive Reynard, it turned out to be a good year. I can't wait for my next race which will be at Brands Hatch.

# CHAPTER 26

## 1985 BBC TV FF2000 GRANDSTAND SERIES

Sponsor and Manager Brian Varney was so delighted with my performances in the 85 formula ford festival that he struck a deal with Rob Cresswell Racing Services to run me in the highly prestigious BBC FF2000 Grandstand series. FF2000 was the next move up the ladder Towards Formula One. Not knowing this at the time, I was about to race against several of the following drivers that made it to Formula One. Mark Blundell, Martin Donelly, Eddie Irvine, John Pratt, Neil Cunningham, Dave Coyne, Ross Hockenhull, Jonathan Bancroft and Benoit Vigneault. All these drivers will be competing in this end-of-year four-race series and I was looking forward to the challenge.

Rob Cresswell felt my smooth driving style would suit the wings and slick tyres that the FF2000 formula use. Even though I did get it wrong on at least one occasion, I put it down to a learning curve. To our delight, Rob was correct and I tested at Brands Hatch in readiness for this series. By the end of the day, I was up in the top four driver lap times. The first round was the following weekend; I was up for it; the Reynard FF2000 was undoubtedly a lovely-looking car, and so was my ff1600 Reynard 84, but the Reynard 84 F2000 looked like a real race car with its wings and wide slick tyres. I finished fourth in the 1985 BBC Grandstand Series. Not bad for the new Boy. Sponsor, Brian Varney. The Team and I were all delighted.

# CHAPTER 27

## 1986 CHAMPION OF BRANDS, BRING IT ON WITH TITLE CONTENDER JAMUN PILOT CHRIS HALL GET READY, RICKY BOY, FOR BATTLES ROYAL

After discussions with several teams, including a couple of outings for a works drive with Van Dieman and Howard Drakes's Laser, we decided to stay with Rob Cresswell; he provides a fabulously prepared car; I've been with him for over a year and won plenty of races in our fantastic Reynard 84, so why change? I remember doing that with Getem, which was not the best decision I ever made.

Brian Varney was still pondering putting me back in an FF2000; I was lucky enough to get runs out in a few FF2000's, which I enjoyed immensely including my run in the ex-Johnny Robinson's Tiga at Silverstone, for which I was very grateful. But in the end, it was ff1600 Champion of Brands; I was well aware that staying at Brands suited Brian and the potential sponsors he may get on board. So, for now, head down and try to keep my new rival for the Champion of Brands Chris Hall, who is quick in the dry and mighty quick in the wet, behind me.

The first round of this twenty-race championship was on the Grand Prix Circuit. It's a driver's dream with super-fast and technical corners like Dingle Dell that you always feel you could have got through quicker,

However, you soon learn you can't. We were with the usual suspects testing mid-week before the race meeting; we were the support race for the Thundersports event. Testing went well. As expected, Chris Hall was well on the pace in his Tony Mundy's designed Jamun. I nicknamed Chris Hall, Albert Hall, after that big building in London. I cut it down to Albi as time passed, but for the moment, we both kept a watchful eye on each other. What a year we are about to have.

Qualifying was on Monday at 11 30 am for this two-day Easter Meeting event. Times were very close. The top ten were covered by just over a second, I claimed pole, Chris Hall second at less than a tenth slower than my good self. Yep, this is going to be fun. The conditions for our race, because it had rained in the afternoon and the rain ceased, left the circuit damp—ideal for Chris Hall. The race for me was disappointing. I made a poor start from pole, Chris got into the first Corner Paddock Hill bend before me. Throughout the race, I was there or thereabouts; I couldn't do anything to beat this maestro. I was now aware I would have a fight on my hands and would have to improve my wet weather driving to allow me to beat him.

We mustn't forget the list of Brands Specialists that help to make up the entry list of twenty-eight drivers. Such as Chris Cresswell, Karl Jones, Chris Ringrose, Len Bull, Paul Sleeman, Johnny Oxborrow, Peter Rogers sister Lucy Rogers, Trevor Farmer Styles, Ted Whitbourne, Bob Hawkins, Bob Lambert, and Rob Murphy in the beloved Getem. There's real talent in this list and I can't wait for the next round of the John Player Formula Ford 1600 Championship on 20th April.

Qualifying. I took the pole for this one, the only driver to get into the 49-second lap with a 49.88. Hall next with a 50.34. Len Bull followed them with 50.51. Next up was the quick Bob Hawkins and the fast-improving Rob Murphy in the Getem.

And now for the Race. Chris Hall and I continued our double act at the head of this race, and Albi made a better start taking the advantage off the line. The race was stopped when two cars needed lifting off the track at

Clearways. On the re-run, I made a better start, letting me assume control of the race. We broke away from the next duel featuring Len Bull's Van Diemen and Bob Hawkins in the Ray with Trever Styles not far behind. Chris and I continued our close battle at the front, giving me my first win in this Championship. The first three drivers make their way up the iron steps to the roof of the Control Tower. Brian Jones, the Voice of Brands, is waiting to interview us. It's always a pleasure to chat with Brian, even more so if you've just won a race. It was good news for the Team and sponsor Brian Varney. Points-wise, Chris and I are joint leaders of the Championship.

# CHAPTER 28

## RAC TOWNSEND FF1600 CHAMPIONSHIP AT BRANDS HATCH.

Brian Varney and Rob Cresswell felt I was ready to show my metal against the big boys in the RAC/Townsend Thoresen race, a support race to the European Grand Prix at the best Circuit in the UK. I was up for it and wanted to see how I would perform in a good ff1600—the Reynard 84, as opposed to the unfortunate Reynard 85. I was nervous, buzzing, excited and quietly hoping I would do well.

I looked at the entry list, it included these drivers:

| | |
|---|---|
| Works Van Diemen | Eddie Irvine and Jason Elliot |
| Works Laser | Fast Peter Rogers |
| Van Diemen | Roland Ratzenberger |
| Reynard | Gerald Van Uitert |
| Van Dieman | Phil Andrews |
| Quest | Gary Ayles |
| Quest | Kenny Brack |
| Van Diemen | Stephen Robertson |
| Van Diemen, | Jeremy Packer |
| Quest | David Germain |
| Van Diemen | Phillippe Favre |
| Quest | Rowan Dewhurst |

Thinks:- I will have my work cut out here.

Qualifying. As usual, I was upfront, having works duo Elliot and Irvine behind me and one to watch fast Peter Rogers behind them. There's something special about FPR; I should imagine a sponsor's dream, out of the car, a true gent. The pit lane marshall gave the signal to start engines; the green flag waved to begin qualifying. I love the roar of the engines. Out we go, and I'm leading this bunch of superstars. I'm hitting the loud pedal a tad early, trying hard to get heat into the tyres; the car feels good; let's see what I can do; surprisingly, already, I've pulled away from the cars behind. I need to relax and continue in the same vein; the pit board on lap three showed I had Pole. I kept the pole for 80% of qualifying, pipped by Jason Elliot on the last lap; I was delighted with that result. I did get a tad excited on the slowing down lap, thinking out loud, I've just beaten all those superstars. Second, on the grid, I will take that.

As I drove back to Rob Cresswell Racings set up in the Paddock, I felt quietly confident, having qualified in front of all these superstars. I was hoping for a good start and a win. I waved to a spectator or two whilst I jogged back to the Paddock; these ff1600 always feel rattly uncomfortable, but once they are flying, it's a beautiful feeling being the pilot of these magnificent machines. As I reached the Teams awning, they were there, Boss Rob and Pipe smoking Dave, with his usual craggy grin, which I grew to like; it was most welcoming. They assisted me to alight out of my beloved Reynad 84; as always, once out, I walked around this fantastic car, patting it here and there. Then it's over to Rob to study the timesheet; it was a glowing report from Rob; his thoughts were the same as mine; ie get a good start, head down and control from the start. That's my mindset for the race; fingers crossed it all goes to plan.

So next was a cuppa made by Pipe Smoking Dave or my wife Anne, who I nicknamed Squidgy yonks ago, well before Princess Diana's Squidgy gate. We have bonded well as a team, which is essential for all of us, and most enjoyable too. The race isn't for a while, it's on the programme for three thirty pm. I tend to want to be alone. All drives are different; mine is to sit in my car, recline the seat and slumber for an hour or so; I don't sleep, chill, I suppose; now and then, I visualize my tactics for the race.

The weather was dry and sunny for the race. Time for all drivers to get kitted up. I don't have any particular way of doing this apart from my red gloves. These are crucial to me; I have won every race whilst wearing these gloves and would be devastated if I lost them. Time to slide down into the cockpit of my beloved Reynard. Always a great feeling, almost theatrical, as if you're preparing for a performance. So here we go, a big one for me. I'm mixing with the big boys, and even if I say so myself, I am doing okay, second on the grid, outside the front row, an excellent place to be so long as you make a good start. Unfortunately I got it wrong; my starts are usually good, but not this time. I was slow off the line ending up third into Paddock Hill Bend's first corner. It was fast and furious. I was on the leading two drivers' heels; at one point, I made a play to get past works Van Diemen driver Jason Elliot for the lead without success. Behind the battles were frantic; between Fast Peter Rogers, Roland Ratzenberger, and Eddie Irvine, inevitably, something had to give; Phil Andrews in his Van Diemen ended up destroyed, which led to a red flag. Race stopped. So a restart. I was happy all the trouble was behind me; I was in third as the Red flag waved, putting me inside the second row. It took a while to sort the track out, but as usual, our fantastic Marshalls did a superb job of getting it ready. The Orange Army has always been outstanding; thank you, Guys and Girls.

Waiting on the grid seems to take forever to get back racing. At last we are underway again, the start Marshall shows a 5-minute warning flag, before the warm-up lap begins. I selected first gear to pull away, then into the second. I tried to select third gear, but it wouldn't come out of second. What a dilemma. I didn't want to dive down the pit lane and retire. I was hoping it would rectify itself; fingers crossed, we were on the first row stuck in second gear hoping for a miracle.

Light comes on and turns green; I get away albeit slowly, cannot select another gear. I have to abort my race by getting into the slip road.

It's very nervy being in this situation. The sound of the engines seemed to magnify whilst twenty-odd ff1600 rush past on their way to Paddock Hill Bend; I was expecting them to come together. Thankfully all the cars managed to roar past me. I was devastated.

Before I could begin worrying, the Orange Army and my team were there; incredibly I had been able to park on the slip road just ahead of the grid; it was an easy exercise to push me well away from danger. Another case of what would have been my chance to shine whilst racing against the best ff1600 drivers in the world failed on the second warming-up lap. Oh well, I will live to fight another day.

John Player Special Champion of Brands. Same weekend, different race. I'm back battling against the Brands specialists. I certainly am not expecting an easy ride, especially from Jamun pilot Chris Albi Hall who is now a championship contender, along with the usual suspects Len Bull, David Germain, John Oxborrow, Paul Sleeman, Trevor Styles, Ted Whitbourne, Bob Hawkins, Ted Hawkins, Bob Lambert, and the fast-improving Rob Murphy in my beloved Getem. I have the benefit of throwing myself into a round of the RAC /Townsend Thoresen ff1600 race and giving me a chance to find out the difference between National and International drivers. I am proud to say I did pretty well.

Qualifying went to plan. I grabbed the pole with a 1 38:06,, Albi Hall 1.39.00, Ted Whitbourne 1 39:01, John Oxborrow 1 39 03. Four-tenths up on Albi, come on, Rick, make a good start, for goodness sake; Mr Hall is tough to pass, he's a great tactician, so Ricky Boy, you need to be on your game when the lights turn green.

In the chat with the Team after Qualifying it was agreed the gearbox problem is no longer an issue, thanks to Guru Rob Cresswell. I'm happy with the car, so as far as I'm concerned no need to touch it. However, Rob and his sidekick Dave will be checking it all over not once, not twice, but several times. True Professionals.

And now for the Race. Hooray, I made a great start dipping into Paddock, ahead of Albi. I love racing against Albi; we are becoming quite a double act. At times, we did get up close and personnel, I can proudly say we never had a coming together; we knew each other's driving technique line, etc. We broke well away from the next duel, which featured Len Bull, and Bob Hawkins, who traded places until Hawkins snatched the initiative with a mile to go. I was delighted to take another win but had to keep a watchful eye on that thorn in my side (only joking, Albi Hall)

The races in 1986 were a dream; I couldn't seem to do anything wrong; The John Player Special Title seemed to be mine. Sadly my car was extensively damaged after being hit from behind during the RAC race supporting the British Grand Prix. Lucky for me, several top manufacturers immediately offered to supply a car for the rest of the season. Brian Varney took up the offer from Van Dieman and a scholar engine. Brian put the Reynard up for sale to help with cash flow. Brian had to try and recoup some of his losses, which I fully understood. The Reynard sold to a Team from Sri Lanka. I was so upset to see it go. A great shame we couldn't have kept it, Brian? However, Rob Cresswell and Pipe Smoking Dave burnt the midnight oil at the Van Dieman factory, to build up a VD For me, and I must agree, it looked great, but it wasn't the Reynard 84. I tried hard to get my beloved Reynard out of my head but couldn't.

Already missing a round of the C.O.B, my next race was in the VD. We shook the car down mid-week to make sure all was good. It felt pretty strange in a different car, but I drove this model at Snetterton when I drove the Works Van Dieman car a few months before. Testing was going well; I soon managed to get down to competitive times.

I felt good in the VD and was ready to give it all. After only a couple of hard laps, the VD broke away as I turned into Paddock, which left me just a passenger in the car. I remember doing my best to correct the situation, but unfortunately, I couldn't do a thing to prevent the VD from going back into the inside tyre wall at the bottom of Paddock.

It wasn't very comforting going backwards, thinking this would hurt. For whatever reason, it seemed to take forever to make contact with the tyre wall; when it did, I stopped in a second, burying the back of the Van

Dieman deep into the tyres. I experienced pain in my neck and chest, which pinpointed something was wrong. We drivers are grateful to our fabulous Marshalls, "The Orange Army." who arrived so quickly to assist me along with the Doctor. It was excruciating getting out of the VD. The Marshalls, guided by a doctor, managed to extrude me from my race car. The Doctor decided not to remove my Crash Helmet just in case of a head injury. I was in quite a bit of pain. The Doctor said I would be, as I have whiplash, which hurts. My chest hurt as I breathed, so it was a visit to St Mary's Hospital. The Team looked very concerned about me; the VD was of secondary concern. I tried to put on a brave face, even though all sorts of things ran through my mind. Such as, I will not be racing this weekend, which means a big points loss; I'm not sure how long I will be out of action until I've been to St Marys.

I was looked after well at St Mary's and had X-rays taken of my head, neck and back. I had suffered whiplash, which meant I needed to wear a collar for at least two week and to make things worse, I had cracked three ribs and was advised not to race for at least a month. Missing three races will mean Chris Hall or the ever-closing Title contender Len Bull could be top of the points table.

My healing process was good. Sadly I did miss three races which put Albi and Bull well in contention for the Title.

And now for my first race in the Van Dieman Scholar. Out in the VD for the first time after my nasty off at Paddock I was not feeling like the old Rick; I was hoping that would soon pass and the old Rick would return. Qualifying, I was pleasantly surprised to be second on the grid. Maybe the old Rick is ok and the nasty accident at Paddock or the worries about finance is locked away.

The Race. I was hoping to do well as the new Sponsor, owner of West Kingsdown Coaches was there. The race was just what I needed. Len Bull led from the start. I stalked him for a few laps, just waiting for an opportunity to get past which happened on the exit of Graham Hill Bend; Len's car got out of line whilst exiting Graham Hill Bend; now my chance to get by, Bull runs wide. I need to get underneath him so I have the line for the entry of the Esses; I'm alongside Len. He's gaining momentum; we are level turning into the Esses; I have the line, Bull has to concede, and I'm through. The race is mine to lose. Thankfully I win—a big smile from me, the Team Brian Varney, and the new Sponsor of West Kingsdown Coaches.

The remainder of the 1986 season was challenging; I continued to have monumental battles with Chris Albi Hall. Len Bull was always there or thereabouts. The John Player Special ff1600 was second best to the International series Townsend Thorensen Championship where I showed I was very competitive, amongst the best. What a year it's been, one I will genuinely never forget.

I fully understood and had an idea that Brian Varney may decide to withdraw his sponsorship. I want to thank you, Brian, for everything you have done over the last few years; without you, Brian, I would not have had the opportunity to reach such a standard as I have without your financial help and guidance and friendship.

# CHAPTER 29

———◆◆◆———

# MORE OF WORKING WITHIN MOTORSPORT

As I've already mentioned, this second book is solely about my years as a race driver and how I became a race instructor at the Brands Hatch Racing School and how I earned a living from the Motorsport Industry.

I wasn't sure when I should write about the piece above, I felt maybe now in the middle of my book would be good; it gives a break from Racing for a while.

1984/85. I became a Brands Hatch Racing Instructor. My first week as a race instructor was making tea and timing the school cars from the control tower. Tony Lanfranci was in charge of running the school. He had a great sense of humour which sometimes upset a few. From the word go, thankfully I seemed to get on well with this big personality of a man. At the time, Tony was probably in his late sixties with a highly chequered career as a race driver. He was still racing saloons, winning and beating drivers a third of his age. Strange, I was now an instructor; just a mere three years earlier I was having the piss taken out of me by the same Lanfranci who was now my boss. Tony continued to bollock and take the piss out of all us instructors. Every day.

The instructors working were all great individuals with big egos, some bigger than others! Here is just a few off the top of my head.

| At number | 1 | Andy Ackerley |
| | 2 | Chris Cresswell |

| | |
|---|---|
| 3 | Johnny Robinson |
| 4 | Peter Townsend |
| 5 | John Penfold |
| 6 | Tim Jones |
| 7 | Peter Rogers |
| 8 | Chris Hall |
| 9 | Tony Trimmer |
| 10 | Les Aga |
| 11 | Gary Ayles |
| 12 | John Penfold |
| 13 | David Germain |
| 14 | Lucy Rogers |
| 15 | Peter Arginsinger |
| 16 | Bill Harry |
| 17 | Heather Bailey |
| 18 | Stuart Cole |
| 19 | Thomas Mezzera |
| 20 | Adrian Fernandez |
| 21 | Jonathan Bancroft |
| 21 | Johnny Mowlem |
| 23 | Rick Shortle |

I had to give up my job as a plasterer, but to be honest, I was so excited to have had the opportunity to become an instructor; plastering never entered my head—Goodbye, dusty work and wet plaster. Guess what? As well as making tea and timing cars from the control tower. Les Aga, yes, Les Aga, the very instructor I had for my initial Trial in the Racing School, was about to instruct me to become an instructor; what are the chances of that happening?

Back in the day, Brands Hatch Racing School were looking for good drivers with personality, and thankfully I had a bit of both.

It was less than a week before I started to get Pupils. I was so bloody nervous with my first Pupils, but quite soon after that, it became easy.

I got on well with the other Instructors, in particular Andy Ackerly, Chris Cresswell, Johnny Robinson, Thomas Mezzera, Tim Jones, Peter Townsend, John Penfold, Bill Harry, well, everyone really.

Some of the other names mentioned earlier hadn't yet become instructors. In fact, by the time they had, I was the instructor that trained them up, as by then, I had moved up to Chief Instructor. The Racing School was extremely busy; you could work at least twenty-eight days a month if you wished. Two to three days a week were Corporate, which was very different. In the eighties, companies used race circuits to entertain their clients and staff. Corporate Events are where Instructors with personalities come to the fore. I would make Andy Ackerly the best, he was quick-witted and great with people, a big Micky taker but done in such a way the clients loved it.

Here are a couple of Ackerly moments that were simply the best. British Airways would do at least two days a week. Their guests were either pilots, Hostesses or top travellers. Having just started as an instructor, I couldn't believe the antics Ackerly and others got up to.to do. I knew of Andy Ackley, He raced ff1600 with Rob Cresswell Racing a few years before I joined them; he then moved on to saloon car racing. Because I was the new Boy at the Race School, Andy would use me as the stooge; I didn't mind at all; it was an ideal way to become accepted. On occasion, the Corporate Groups gather above the start-finish in the gantry viewing area and look down on us instructors in the pit lane whilst we look up to the guests to introduce ourselves. I felt something was going to happen, Andy was standing close, it was time for Andy to introduce himself. He put his arm around me, pulled me in tight, and said "My name is Andy Ackerly, this is Rick Shortle, and what are we here for, Boys?" There's a little pause, followed by "To pull the Birds." He then repeats the same thing expecting us to join in, "which we do." I could feel myself going red as a beetroot; I certainly couldn't see Present Circuit owner Johnathon Palmer allowing that today.

On another Corporate day, a group from British Airways gathered in the pitlane waiting for Tony Lanfranci to inform them which instructor and car to go in. All of a sudden, prancing along the gallery above was Andy Ackerly, dressed like Super Man. Our Race suits are Blue, cleverly; he wore a red pair of underpants over his race suit, finished off with a red Super Man effect scarf. He looked amazing. So there we all were, Clients and Instructors mesmerised with Ackerly making his way across the gantry and down the iron stairs whilst doing all the Super Man moves. The British Airways guests, Instructors and Marshalls gave him such applause. What a way to start a Corporate event!

I've only been here five minutes and can't believe the difference between working as a plasterer and being a race instructor. It certainly feels unreal. The days were long and hard. As a new Boy, I loved it. Back then, apart from the Corporate Events, which were great fun, and usually fronted by the Voice of Brands, the one and only Brian Jones. It was predominantly a race School that urged pupils to progress to a good enough standard to try their hand at motor racing. I'm so grateful to John Webb for considering me as an Instructor. Now I am an instructor; I try my best to do a good job, which helps me to climb the instructor ladder.

# CHAPTER 30

## BRIAN JONES THE ONE AND ONLY VOICE OF BRANDS HATCH.

### "HIGH WIDE AND HANDSOME"

As mentioned earlier in the book, Brian Jones owned M.R.S Motor Racing Stables' before it became Brands Hatch Racing School. Brians's face was prevalent during my first couple of years as an instructor; he ran the Corporate Events and odd manufacturer days. Brian liked instructors to comment on the analyst sheet, funny, sarcastic or, at times, even complementary. We would all give it a try. I seemed to be quite good, particularly with taking the mickey. Brian used my comments a lot, which gave me a few brownie points, "creep." I was also doing well in ff1600, which the Race School liked, and they could use this as a push for the School, ie Ex Brands Hatch Racing Pupil, leading the ff1600 John Player Special Champion of Brands and also now an instructor at The Brands Hatch Racing School. Being on the podium most weekends at Brands meant Brian Jones interviewed me regularly, which helped us get to know each exceptionally well. Brian would tell the corporate clients a little about me and then explain that I would give them a briefing on lines, flags and safety before they go down to the circuit to drive the saloons and single-seaters. I would be available to drive them for a couple of laps in the D-Type Jaguar.

I felt thrilled with my progress; I had fitted in well with the other instructors. I understood the job, finding it enjoyable and rewarding.

Quite quickly, I was offered work from Brian Jones's Events, mainly Austin Rover. These days were brilliant; three days of taking clients around Brands Hatch Indi Circuit at speed was magic. Brian invited top drivers of the time to work on these days. The likes of Nigel Mansel, yes Nigel Mansel, Steve Soper, Tiff Needell, Tim Jones and Rick Shortle.

John Thomlinson had masterminded a skid car; it could replicate all types of sliding, from understeer to oversteer to downhill on ice. John had a little area in the paddock set up as a twisty track; the clients would try to negotiate around it without knocking down the oil drums that lined the track. John sat in the passenger seat with his magic box on his lap. A couple of dials, when turned, will tell the car to understeer, oversteer or be on the ice. John Thomlinson coaxed Nigel Mansell to have a go during the lunch break. Nigel was up for it and was bloody useless, knocking over most of the oil drums as he bashed his way around the skid track. It was hilarious; fair play to Nigel, he took it all in good fun. The Brian Jones days were great fun, and I'm still pinching myself doing what I'm doing.

# CHAPTER 31

## WELCOME, JACKY AND ISABEL EPSTEIN

Jackie and Isabel Epstein were amazing to work for; by the time they took over from MRS "Motor Racing Stables", I was up to speed with it all and soon upgraded to a Senior Instructor.

Jackie was an ex-F5000 driver whilst Isabel was in Marketing. We noticed from the offset how things at the race school began to change, without taking away the fun aspect. I got on well with Jackie and Issy. The School was busier than ever, wages were good, and I was happy. Being happy prevented me from worrying about finding a budget for 1987. I was trying to find another sponsor to replace Brian Varney, which will be almost impossible.

It wasn't long after Jackie and Issy took over that they called me into the office to inform me I was now the chief instructor, increasing my daily rate. I was delighted they felt I deserved it. With it came responsibilities, such as training any new Instructors, which was fine by me, and I had to set the standard as an Instructor. Issy explained that the Race School is busier than ever; it seems some of our instructors are doing work for other Race Circuits that have cottoned on to how Brands Hatch operates.

Over the years as an instructor, I trained up a few to become instructors, that's for sure; the most difficult one must have been the most annoying, difficult, awkward sod by the name of Gary Ayles. He's a lovely fellow, apart from being an annoying – difficult-awkward sod. I've repeated it; if you are reading this, Gary, you know that is true.

During my time as an Instructor, I had the privilege to give tuition to many celebrities, some memorable, others a pain in the arse. Here are just a few in no particular order.

Eddie Kid. Motor Cycle Stunt Rider. All sorts of things were going through my mind as Tony Lanfranci introduced me to Eddie. My first impressions were good; he was polite, intelligent and good-looking. I spent a week with him, about a couple of hours a day, and I enjoyed working with Eddie. He was completely different to what I felt he might have been like; he listened to me and did what I asked of him; everything was inch perfect.

By the end of the week, Eddie was quick, smooth and consistent; I wished him well for the coming race. It wasn't long after I worked with Eddie that he had a horrific accident whilst preparing to do a jump at a big show in Stratford upon Avon. Sadly, he was left paralysed.

Lost in the Desert Mark Thatcher. As I arrived at the pit lane, I did the usual thing, sit in the Porta Cabin where our Instructors congregated until we got orders from TL. It seemed different to usual; Tony was not quite as loud as expected. It wasn't long before I was called to the Control Tower. I got the usual abuse from the rest of the Instructors to get working, etc, which is too rude for me to include in this book. So off I trot up the steel staircase to the Control Tower. As I entered, I saw a couple of heavies looking like minders, and I wasn't far wrong; that's what they were. There was a well-dressed Lady with them and I discovered she was Mark Thatcher's millionaire wife from Dallas, Texas, Diane Burgdorf. Tony called me over and politely and quietly explained what was going to happen. Tony said "We have our Prime Minister, Margaret Thatcher, and her son, Mark Thatcher, waiting in the Atlantic Suite. Mark is here today to brush up on his Race Craft. You are going to be his instructor". I made my way back to the control Tower and waited for Mr Thatcher to arrive, which he did quite a while later in a big black limousine.

I was standing there like a spare prick at a wedding, waiting for Mr Thatcher to appear; at bloody last, he stepped out of his Limo suited and booted in his race gear. Was I looking forward to this? Was I buggery? I did my best to do an in-car briefing; Mark just wanted to get on with it and suggested I did a few laps first to give him an idea of lines, braking gear etc. which we did, but it was all in vain. Without much luck, I did my best for the next hour to try and get him to understand that he had this terrible way of driving which created chronic understeer. When I explained what he was doing, he replied yes, I know! that's always been my problem. If he had paid a bit more attention to what I was telling him his technique might have been much improved. I thanked the sweet Lord when it was over; I escorted Mark up to the control tower; he then went out for some solo laps—giving me a chance to have a word in TL's ear; he told me, no problem, you coped well. Whilst doing his solo laps, Mark, as expected, had a few excursions to the grass, thankfully, there was no damage to Mark or the car.

Bobby Moore is a Footballer. Captain of England's 1966 World Cup Winners. What a fabulous guy; he would come into our Porta Cabin for a laugh and joke, nothing cocky about him; it was a pleasure to have been able to sit alongside this great man. One of my favourite memories.

George Sewell was a Detective in the 1970s programme Special Branch. George comes across as a hard-as-nails detective; he looked hard too. I went to meet him and shook his hand; he immediately said, Rick, I'm shitting myself; please go easy with me. I've learned to ignore that statement. I've heard it that many times, and when they get into a car, they try to show off and go too fast, too soon. However, that wasn't the case with George. He was shitting himself, and he didn't want to drive. I asked if he would like me to drive him around, he quickly answered yes, please, but go easy with me. I respected his wish and did a few laps, which he loved. Thanks, George. It was a pleasure. Whenever I see him on TV, I think of his day at Brands. There were many others who joined us for a days driving,including Les Ferdinand, Sylvia Simms, Frankie goes to Hollywood, Chief Minister of the Isle of Man, Derek Daley, the cast of Coronation Street, several MPs, the list goes on.

In late 1986, The Racing School was extremely busy. I spent quite a portion of my time training more instructors such as David Germain, Lucy Rogers, Thomas Mazzera, Jonathon Bancroft, Johnny Mowlem, to name a few.

We all had an hour for dinner; I would prefer mine late because the afternoon goes quicker, and most of us would take our school car to the Kentagon restaurant to chill for an hour. On this particular occasion, as I walked back to my car, a guy rolled up on a mean-looking motorbike; he pulled up by my side. It wasn't until he took his helmet off that I realised who it was, only my arched rival Chris Albi Hall. By then, we had stopped racing against each other as had I decided to move on and leave ff1600, hopefully racing something else in 1987. We started chatting. I asked Chris what he was doing at Brands; he said "I was hoping to find someone to guide me to the person that Hires and Fires Racing Instructors". I said, slightly showing off, "I can help; park your bike and come with me". I took Chris to meet the Boss, Isabel Epstein; Her office was just fifty yards away. I told Chris, "You stay outside. I will pop in and see her". I chatted with Issy; she remarked that if he's good enough for you, then he's good enough for us. Job done. I went out and grabbed Chris and took him to introduce himself to Isabel; with that, he got the job, and I trained him up the following week. I have to say Chris Hall was a superb Instructor; Chris has always maintained it changed his world for the better. Since then, we have become best buddies and not arch rivals.

Chris, with my guidance, soon became a Senior Instructor; we worked well. Issy Epstein noticed that, and it wasn't before too long we began to get most of the exciting jobs For example, we spent a whole day with stars of Coronation Street, Kevin Webster and Stuart Wolfenden. who ran the garage on the Street. Kevin is still there. Coronation Street was doing a piece on Banger Racing, ITV arranged for these likely lads to spend a day at the School; Chris and I were asked to put them through the school, hopefully giving them a better idea. We had a fabulous time, spending an hour or two in the Thistle Hotel at the entrance to the circuit.

# CHAPTER 32

## NEW RACE CARS TO BE BUILT AT BRANDS HATCH

Brain Child of John Webb and Jacky Epstein,. three new marques were about to be built. The Multi-Sport is a two-seater open-topped sports car, a single-seater called the Formula First, aimed at the true amateur, ideal to try single-seaters before stepping into the cut and thrust of ff1600. Finally, the Formula Forward, a winged car with Slick tyres, again aimed at drivers that wish to experience winged vehicles at a cost that would be much more competitive than any of the established Formula's

I was involved in developing these marques. Brands Hatch Racing entered Andy Ackerly, Chris Cresswell and Gary Ayles into a Formula First Sprint race. It was early 1987, and I shared the car with Chris. We finished second in class, which boded well for its debut later that year. Being a starter Formula, it did attract lousy driving and quite spectacular crashes. Heather Bailey was very quick but had quite a few comings together; thankfully, she lived to tell the tale. Ben Edwards went on to win the Championship sponsored by my ex-sponsor, Legal Services. Although designed to be a low-cost two-seater sports car, the Multi-Sport never took off. Therefore the Multi-Sport was used mainly as a Corporate passenger rides car which turned out to be ideal for this purpose. I've completed more joy laps in this car than I care to remember

Finally, helping to develop the Formula Forward is something not to be forgotten. I had spent an afternoon going around the circuit, coming in after a few laps to report and chat about this new winged car with Jacky Epstein. The last outing of the day I will never forget. The moment I started to improve my speed, the car felt very light with no grip, which was somewhat strange, as it was fine up to then. As I dipped into the esses, the car started to fly and somehow took off and landed on top of the Armco, rocking backwards and forwards. Knowing I never made any mistakes, I was hoping to find out what went wrong. Problem solved. Jackie had been standing at the Esses, watching how the Formula Forward looked through that section. Luckily he was watching the car as it dipped into the Esses. He watched it lift and begin to fly; at that moment, positioned on South Bank, the information board went down precisely at the same time I flew off. It was a freak gust of wind that caused both issues. It was the start of the great storm of 1987, which caused terrible damage to the British Isles a few hours later.

Sadly these Marques raced for a while but fizzled out.

# CHAPTER 33

## FUN AND FROLICS AT THE RACE SCHOOL

The bottoms-up section.

On more than a few occasions, an instructor or instructors like to mess around. I won't bore you with countless stories of silly instructors being downright daft and sometimes dangerous, and please excuse me if you find them rude, which some are hilarious, just the same.

On one occasion my now best mate Chris Hall was in charge of the Control Tower, Tim Jones and I were on flag duty at Druids, and all seemed fine, in fact, quite dull. Until David Germain decided to do something silly, I suspect it was because Tony Lanfraci was not available that day; we all took turns on these occasions to run the Tower. Today it just happened to be Chris Hall's turn. Tim and I stood on the outside of Druids, picking a good vantage point to be able to spot any wrong or dangerous driving. After a spate of nothing, we could see a school car driven by Germain; his vehicle seemed to wander from side to side, and we had no idea why. As Germain approached the entry to Druids, he was in a bizarre position in the car; we hadn't a clue what was going on until he was coming to the exit of Druids when he had somehow managed to get his Arse out of the passenger window. Tim and I laughed so much that we had tears in our eyes. We could see he was in trouble; David Germain had gotten into such a tight position in the car that he could not turn the steering wheel or lift the throttle. The School car hit the barriers infield, bouncing off, aiming him and the vehicle at the barriers on the outside.

Tim and I managed to extrude Germain from the car, checking he was ok. The car was just about driveable, so I told him to slowly drive back to the Control Tower and explain what happened to Chris, "God Knows" what he told him, but I believe when Issy heard about it he was suspended for a month or two.

This one is all about timing, at which Tim Jones was ACE. He had to know when the correct type of fart was ready to be released - I still don't know the right kind. Tim would stretch himself out on one of the Benches in the Porta Cabin and have a box of matches in his hand.

Tim had this down to a fine art, we would watch in anticipation, studying his technique. Then all of a sudden, he would pull a strange face, then let rip with a cracker of a fart that sounded like it was travelling at high speed. The timing is critical. When to strike the match. Tim gets the timing right nine times out of ten. He strikes the match having made sure his School race uniform is extremely tight around his arse, which lets the fart through more straightforwardly and faster. Perfection as the match strikes a lovely flame; the fart Ignites, sending a magnificent flame from his backside almost to the back of his knees. A big round of applause, then back to work.

Rick Shortle and the Circuit Radio.

We always had a Circuit radio in the Porta Cabin, which would drive us all mad. All we heard all day was Lanfranci calling us to come to the control tower or stand by our cars; they were on their way. We got to know him and didn't worry too much when he told us they were on their way. We would turn the radio down or even off sometimes. On one occasion, when we were all in the Porta Cabin, I decided enough was enough. Lanfranci was belting out nonsense messages; I shouted to the Instructors, Right, I've had enough; I grabbed the Circuit Radio telescopic aeriel, walked casually to the loos and I placed the radio in the toilet and then flushed the chain. About half a dozen instructors cramped behind me to see me in action. I got the usual round of applause for being a rebel.

Back to Front.

Here's a trick we would play on pupils; it didn't always work but seemed to work more often than not. It was all about how you handed them the open-faced crash helmet, ie back to front. The Pupil, nine times out of ten, would put it on their head the wrong way round; we only did this if we thought they were up for a laugh. The Pupil would often arrive with a crash hat already on the wrong way around; we had to tell them for safety reasons.

Bogus Pupil.

Now and then, we would play a game with one of the new instructors and sometimes even with an existing Instructor. We would dress up, maybe even put a false beard on, hoping the Instructor doesn't know us; we found it better to do it with a new Instructor, as they would hopefully have less chance of recognising us. The bogus Pupil would appear very nervous and fidgety; when told to drive out to the circuit, the bogus Pupil did so with some trepidation. It was a plodding half a lap; the instructor tried to egg the bogus pupil on, and with that, the fake pupil put the pedal to the metal and appeared to drive like a lunatic; the instructor was terrified and ordered the bogus driver back to the pit lane. Once in the pit lane, the bogus pupil is ordered to report to the chief Instructor.

It must have seemed strange for the new instructor to see quite a few instructors milling around. They were waiting to see the instructor's reaction when he discovered the bogus pupil was an instructor playing a game on him? It was a bit of an initiation ceremony to welcome them to BHRS. We all laughed and hugged the new instructor. I patted him on the back and said "You've passed. Welcome to the Brands Hatch Racing School."

# CHAPTER 34

## HOVERCRAFT PILOT

During a lunchtime break in the Kentagon, Circuit owner John Webb beckoned me; he was in his usual place far right of the bar, perched on a bar stool with a cigar almost as big as himself hanging out of his mouth. When J W beckons you, you go!

J W asked if I knew that the Brands Hatch days offer Hovercraft Flying Experiences, run by Ray Allen. I said that I did and he then asked me if I would be interested in becoming a Hovercraft Pilot; I thought another string to my bow, so why not? let's give it a go; nothing ventured, nothing gained. J W was pleased and set a training day for Ray Allen to train me up to a suitable standard. I was looking forward to meeting Ray Allen (never met him before). A few days later, I met Ray, a smashing bloke. Working with Ray was a laugh a minute and I enjoyed working alongside Ray but hated everything about flying a Hovercraft; I never felt in control. As far as I was concerned, the hovercraft had a will of its own, and I was bloody useless. I had to tell J W becoming a Hovercraft pilot wasn't for me, he was okay about it and thanked me for trying it out.

It wasn't long before they enlisted another more suitable guy, a chap named Steve Treacher or Treacle, as we called him. Treacle turned out to be a first-class Hovercraft Pilot and a circuit instructor.

# CHAPTER 35

# WORKING AT THE IDEAL HOME EXHIBITION LONDON

John Webb has had a stand at the Ideal Home Exhibition in London every Christmas for the last couple of years; it seemed only a select few would get a chance to work there; this is the type of Show, if you are prepared to work hard, the rewards should come.

When I got wind of the show, I put my name down to work on it. By chance, one of the selected few couldn't make the show. It was American Peter Argetsinger; I was invited to take his place for the show; all I had to do now was sell well.

The BHRS Stand was simple: the usual promotional pictures, leaflets and a single-seater school car. Each of the five sellers had a podium to work from. Our job was to sell the Racing School "Initial Trial", it was simple in theory but quite challenging for some instructors. We would ask for a fiver deposit for an initial trial; the Customer would get a Brands Hatch Tee Shirt and a guaranteed place at the Race School. We were allowed to keep the fiver deposit. To most of the team, the fiver seemed so small, and the thoughts were negative about making money. I could see it as an excellent little earner; (Dell Boy). I was determined to give it a go.

My first day was a learning day, I worked hard on getting my sales pitch slick. Once you've got a good sales pitch, you're half way there. I soon learned to be pleasant, not try too hard, and most of all, believe in the product, which I did. Not to be too big-headed, I somehow found selling an Initial trial for the BHRS a challenge, enjoyable, bloody hard work and extremely rewarding. My first day was a long one. I got to the Ideal Home Exhibition Brands Hatch Racing School stand early! It was new to me; I wanted to feel what it would be like to see so many people milling around. Being inquisitive, I wondered why John Webb chose the Ideal Home Exhibition. I soon found it evident that Christmas was just around the corner, ie, an ideal Christmas Present. I watched the other instructors, getting an idea of how they were doing; some seemed to get fed up quickly, periodically leaving their Podium for a cuppa or a skive. Lofty (Stewart Cole), one of the old School, wouldn't move; he kept selling and did well. A couple of Instructors were good. American Peter Argetsinger and Heather Bailey. Heather was particularly impressive but a little too greedy; her technique was to get as many people around her podium in the hope she would get big numbers; this very rarely works; I found twos and threes to be best. I soon realised most visitors would browse for the first couple of hours, and they would look around for freebies, ie, carrier bags, stickers, pens, etc. By midday, the visitors were ready to chat and hopefully buy.

My first day of selling exceeded all my hopes and expectations, I knew I had sold the most Initial Trials. I was crafty, when the other instructors asked how I was doing, I would reply with a much lower figure than I had actually sold. Within a few days, the other instructors had twigged I was selling quite a bit more than them and couldn't understand why I wasn't in a hurry to rush in the following day.

Lofty was always first on the stand before the Show opened. Guess what? he and most of the other Instructors had this mad idea that my Podium was the magic Podium. Hence the following morning, they would all rush to pinch the podium I was on the previous day; bloody hilarious. The Show ran for a couple of weeks, I outsold every other Instructor every day of the show, and I was simply the best.

I was lucky enough to work at the Ideal Home Exhibition for Brands Hatch until they decided not to use it anymore.

It was a fantastic cash bonus for the time of the year when the cold wintery month of December is a poor earner at the Brands Hatch Racing School. I hope it will also help me get similar work from motor manufacturers in the future.

# CHAPTER 36

## 1987 NO SPONSORSHIP

After losing my sponsorship deal with Brian Varney at the end of 1986, to continue racing, I had to search for sponsorship, which wasn't going to be easy.

If there's one thing I'm good at is never giving in, I have always said if you want something enough, don't give up; it will happen.

I did a few press releases to the local press, AutoSport and Motoring News, explaining my options for 1987. My first choice was FF2000 with Rob Cresswell Racing Services. Although no other team could match their budget, I hadn't got a chance of raising the amount required to join Rob's team.

My next choice was to try something very different, Sports 2000, which was dominated by two remarkable drivers at the top of their game. In the Shrike, the one and only Ian Flux (Fluxie) and in the Royale, Mike Fullma Taylor works drivers for the marques they drove.

I had watched a couple of races and fancied having a crack at it. Taylor and Fluxie were night and day quicker than the rest of the drivers; it was apparent they were the ones to beat.

I hadn't a clue who to contact, so I went with the car I liked the look of best, which was the Royal driven by Mike Fullma Taylor. I rang Alan Cornock, Boss of the Royal Sports 2000, and as previously mentioned,

Boss of the Royal ff1600 driven by Rick Morris. It seemed the best option for me.

Up to now, I didn't know Fluxie or Taylor; I got to know Fluxie very well over the coming years; if I had known Fluxie then, I would have loved to race in his team.

Ian Flux's team got in touch with me and tried to tempt me to race with them; sadly, I had already struck a deal with Royal, something now I regret, as I'm sure it would have been one hell of an experience both on and off the circuit.

I was going to struggle with the budget but still felt I would find it somewhere, somehow. Although Brian Varney had stopped sponsoring me, he did help me a little. I managed to get Sealink on board, which became a nightmare, and West Kingsdown Coaches.

Long time friend and motor racing nut Ken Hall was tremendous help with promotional and marketing work.

# CHAPTER 37

## WOW, THANKS, MR WEBB

After being called into Circuits owner John Webb's office, I somehow knew he was aware I was struggling to raise a 1987 budget.

I met John in his office. It was pretty early in the day; I will never forget he asked if I would like a drink, which I refused. With that, he slid his hand to the back of an ornament on the sideboard bringing out what looked like a massive glass of scotch. John raised his glass and said cheers; I must admit to being somewhat confused about where this conversation may be going.

J.W. blurted out, " Rick, I will finance your racing for the foreseeable future so long as you continue to seek further support yourself". I was gobsmacked. For once, this wasn't by chance; it was because I had impressed J.W. in my racing, became a good instructor and sold well at the Ideal Home Exhibition. It was of those "I don't believe it" moments. One thing about John Webb is that he's a man that is true to his word and he was. Thank you, John.

John Webb continued to sponsor me, together with my co driver, the great Lady racer Davina Galicia, in the Thundersports Series. (Look up The Forgotten Drivers of F1). John supported me until I was fortunate enough to find my own sponsorship.

# CHAPTER 38

## 1987 BRANDS HATCH LEISURE - BRITISH SPORTS 2000 CHAMPIONSHIP

Round 1 on Brands Hatch G.P. circuit. Not much to shout about, usual suspects Taylor and Fluxie on the front row with me third inside the second row; I haven't disgraced myself; I'm happy with third on the grid; my job now is to hang onto or maybe try to hang onto these giants of Sports 2000.

The start was good. I pulled away with Fluxie and Mike Taylor. Christ, they are quick in these big cars. Compared with my blessed Reynard 84, these things feel like a tank. I followed them around the GP Circuit but knew I would never keep up with the pace; I was in a comfortable third place. Third place, first race, was respectable. Mike and Fluxie cleared off into the distance, leaving me in a lonely race. At least I got to ride in the lap of honour car for my third place in the race.

Next Race is at Thruxton, I can't wait, I've never been there. Thruxton circuit is so unlike Brand Hatch, with its super-fast sweeping bends which are taken flat out for the brave, plus two technical sections, the first section is after a fast wide right-hand corner Allard, which then goes left and flat, followed by specialised area Campbell-Cobb and Segrave, which is so easy to overcook. Lots of time is lost here if you get it wrong. The successive corners, Noble, Goodwood, Village and Church, as I said, are flat out for the brave, watching out for the Marshall's post on the clipping point at Goodwood. I got reported for using too much kerb there; for being inches from the Marshalls heavily tyred post. Sorry Marshalls. That section keeps you alert. It's a fabulous section; the car goes light, and it's important to be smooth and gentle with the race car.

It's now flat out through Brooklands, a very gentle curve that brings you to Club Chicane. It's fantastic as you turn the car left and right to exit. The exit goes over the back of the Start Finish Line, with the chequered flag waved just before the entrance to the first corner Allard. So all I have to do is get it right.

Thruxton Qualifying. I invited sponsors Brian Varney and Sealink. Strange how things seem to go wrong when you ask sponsors along.

Midweek testing went well; I still couldn't match Taylor or Fluxies lap times; my times were promising and looking like another third place in the bag. Which was a good feeling; at least I stamped my authority on the third podium spot. Qualifying was dry. We had the garages, which is always a bonus. Especially when sponsors are present, it helps make them feel a little more special.

Qualifying begins; I try to tuck in behind teammate Mike Fullma Taylor, which at the moment feels easy, simply because we are doing a couple of slow laps to bed in the new slick tyres.

Lap three, here we go. I managed to hang onto Mike over the start-finish line through Allard, and amazingly through the Campbell-Cob-Seagrave section, it felt bloody hairy.

I was still with Mike in the flat-out Noble section, followed by Goodwood, remembering the Marshalls Post; as I exited the clipping point, I felt the car go light; within a flash, I was just a passenger in the Royal. Luckily spinning away from the circuit, it felt so f.....g fast I just waited for the bang. No bang. I managed to stop the Royal 2000 before that happened. What a bummer! Three laps, no lap time of any use.

I was disappointed to have lost control but delighted it wasn't a driver error; the rear bodywork had decided to unlock itself. It caused a tremendous loss of grip on the rear of the S2000. Once that happened, I was just a passenger in the car.

We waited for the qualifying sheets to arrive, only to inform us what we already knew. I was the slowest of everyone. Therefore it was the back of the grid for me, with twenty-eight cars ahead; this race would give me an idea of how good I would be against the other drivers, going to have to fight my way through. Taylor and Flux will be long gone.

The Fullma Racing Team cobbled the rear-section together the best they could, making it safe for the race but looking very second-hand.

Mike Taylor remarked he expected me to get third place in the race. Bloody hell putting me under a bit of pressure there, Mr Taylor. My thoughts were the same; I had already felt I could finish third, a tall order from the back of the grid. I'm certainly up for that.

Now for the race. I have a 30-minute race to claim third place and make the podium; unlike the first race at Brands, which was a bit lonely, I will be busy overtaking plenty of cars this time. I enjoyed the race, it was great fun working my way through the field and I managed third place, got a pat on the back from Mike Fullma Taylor, third place on the podium with superstars Fluxie / Taylor, plus a ride in the lap of honour car. All in all, the day ended up well.

My first season in Sports 2000 continued to be good fun, but sadly I was unable to match Flux and Taylor; I could say the obvious, they have been racing Sports 2000 for some time, and they are at the top of their game. The honest answer is they were better than me.

As well as contesting the 1987 Sealink Ferries Sports 2000 Championship, I was lucky enough to race in the 1987 Thundersports. My Co-Driver was Davina Galica who was the sixth fastest person on skies in the world, having clocked a staggering 120mph at Les Arcs, France, narrowly missing the woman's world record. Davina's first race was at Brands Hatch; she flew to Brands fresh from her record attempt to share the driving of the Royal RP42 Sports 2000. Davina is a very accomplished competitive driver; we got on extremely well, very professional and always good for a laugh. I enjoyed my time with Davina, we still keep in touch.

The Sports 2000 championship continued to stay the same, with Taylor and Fluxie fighting for the lead, leaving me to pick up the third spot. I finished third in the Championship, which wasn't bad for my first attempt. I wouldn't contest this series in 1988 as I want to try something else. Funds permitting!

# CHAPTER 39

## SALOONS FOR ME IN 1988

In November 1987, by chance, Former Surtees F1 team manager Peter Briggs had a conversation with me, having read I was looking to change to Saloon car racing. Peter Briggs explained that he would run three cars in the 1988 Honda CRX Challenge, the latest saloon car one-make series, which was proving an ideal platform for manufacturers to show their latest vehicles to potential customers. He asked me if I would like to join his team as one of his drivers. I was amazed and excited to join a race team run by such a prestigious owner. All I needed to do now was find a budget.

Peter told me that there would be two more drivers in the team and he said that Andy Ackerley and Tim Lee Davey would be joining me. Well, I was shocked, extrovert Andy Ackerley (remember his antics at Brands?) has raced saloons for a couple of years after a highly successful time in ff1600. The winner of the TV series Big Time, Tim Lee Davey, came across as highly professional. Tim went on to race in world Sports Cars and Le Mans. He's put himself under a heap of pressure with his press release explaining he's only in the championship to win a Honda CRX, which is part of the prize money for the winner to give his wife as a Christmas present, he will soon find out it's not going to be a walkover. (Tim was mentioned in my book earlier on); he was one of the Brands Hatch Racing Instructors when I was a pupil. Yep, I'm still pinching myself.

I soon discovered that the highly prestigious Honda CRX Challenge had attracted all the one-make saloon car specialists.

Here are a few names; I'm sure those who follow the one-make series will know the following characters—all entered to race in the 1988 Honda CRX Challenge.

Patrick Watts
Barrie Wizzo Williams
Rob Hall
Tim Sugden
Graham Churchill
Russell Grady
Paul Taft
Dave Carvell
Dave Loudoun
Steve Waudby
Andy Ackerley
Tim Lee Davey

I did quite a lot of research, including watching videos of these drivers, my first impression was that they are bloody lunatics, second thought is that I have a lot to learn.

# CHAPTER 40

# CANTERBURY MORTGAGE CENTRE AND JEREMY AXWORTHY

By Chance, whilst approaching companies for much-needed sponsorship, I came upon Atlas Car Hire, which had just opened a Branch in Ashford Kent, just a few miles from my home in Sellindge.

In those days, I never bothered writing proposals; I would puff myself up, walk in, and ask to speak to the owner. If I managed to get that far, I would have a proposal to let them know what I had on offer.

It was a numbers game with plenty of knockbacks; I felt I dealt well with that. After all, they can only say no. Most of the time, I chose car-related companies.

Atlas Car Hire fitted the bill, and by chance, the first person I spoke to was the Owner, a very loud and somewhat excitable Mr Jeremy Axworthy. I briefly introduced myself and told him why I wanted to talk to him. He invited me to his office for a chat; I never realised Mr Axworthy could talk the hind leg off a donkey. We all know the type they can speak forever without mentioning the sponsorship I'm seeking.

As I've been in this situation before, I learned to be patient and let the potential sponsor carry on and wait for the outcome; sponsorship is bloody hard to come by, and I'm more than prepared to wait. I must have been in his office for a couple of hours; still no mention of sponsorship; he then suggested we nip down to the pub for a beer; by now, I was thinking is this going somewhere? Or should I give an excuse to leave him with the information to dwell over it? I decided to stick with it, go to the pub, and see the outcome. As we entered, there were a few people he knew. Immediately he held court by saying this is Rick Shortle, the local race driver. My company, Atlas Car Hire, are going to sponsor him. As a result, he wanted to keep me in suspense, and I was sure he had already decided in his office whilst we were chatting that it would be his plan, to show off in front of a few acquaintances in the pub.

All I needed to know was how much sponsorship it would be. I was now buzzing with excitement. Jeremy Axworthy invited me to take a seat to discuss his sponsorship plans. Jeremy went on to say his sponsorship plans were not for money. Atlas Car Hire is a new company that needs every penny for the business but he is prepared to supply me with two road cars, one for me and one for Anne. He will also try to raise or introduce me to some of his clients who may be interested in sponsorship.

For me, that was a good day's work. Let's hope Mr Axworthy is true to his word, I have two road cars and another potential sponsor to help fund my Honda CRX Challenge car with Peter Brigg's Edenbridge Honda Team.

Jeremy Axworthy got the ball rolling when we arrived back at his office and true to his word, Anne and I had a road car each; just a week later. Within another week, Jeremy had news releases in all the local newspapers stating he would sponsor me in the 1988 Honda CRX Challenge. A few weeks down the line, he booked a stand in the Ashford Enterprise Show and he commissioned Gina Campbell, Donald Campbell's daughter and myself to chat with and promote Atlas Car Hire, which was most enjoyable.

My other concern was funding for this year's Honda CRX race programme. Again Jeremy came good; he had arranged for me to meet a couple of high flyers that had recently formed their own Mortgage Company, "The Canterbury Mortgage Company". I went to their Canterbury offices to meet the principals by the names of Mike and

Shaun. They loved the idea of promoting their Mortgage business through motor racing, which I found somewhat strange, but I kept that to myself.

I came away having struck a deal for them to sponsor me in the 1988 Honda CRX Challenge. We shook hands. I let Mike and Shaun know that Peter Briggs would be in touch to set up a meeting to cross the Eyes and dot the T's. A very prestigious championship and I will be out of my comfort zone, but I was looking forward to the challenge. Well, Jeremy Axworthy, I am so glad I continued to listen to you gabbling away back in your office a few weeks ago.

The only saloons cars I have raced were the racing school cars in Celebrity races, which were great fun. My only claim to fame in those was to smash the lap record set by Mclaren F1 driver John Watson by over half a second. I have no allusions to setting the world alight in my first year of saloon car racing; however, am I looking forward to it? You bet I am, especially with Andy Ackerley and Tim Lee Davey as teammates in such a prestigious team. I can't wait.

The Canterbury Mortgage Centre invited Anne and me to a few pre-season meals in lovely Restaurants. They were fabulous evenings. We soon became good friends who were looking forward to an enjoyable racing season.

Canterbury Mortgage Centre were friends with Bob Matthews, the UK's fastest long-distance blind runner who would be running in the Para Olympics in Seoul and is trying to raise funding to compete there.

We put our heads together and came up with a challenge for Bob Matthews to drive me around Brands Hatch in my Honda CRX race-prepared Hot Hatch. I asked Peter Briggs if they could fit a passenger seat for me to give Bob instruction and help around the Brands Hatch 2.4 mile Indy Circuit. Peter was more than happy to arrange it. We manage to get ITV to film it and give us a slot on the evening news. Bob Matthews was up for it, and so was I; it was an experience I will never forget; I wasn't scared, concerned or worried. It was a marvellous experience. Bob got me to drive him around slowly, explaining everything - Trees, bridges, track deviations etc. Now it was Bob's turn. With the ITV cameraman in the back filming; I gave Bob a briefing explaining I would instruct without holding the steering wheel and hoping we would reach a speed of 60 mph over the start-finish line. Bob asked me to give instructions quietly so he could sense the bridges, trees, contours etc. Bob was excellent; he reached a speed of 65mph. We managed to get a slot for Bob to carry out this Challenge during the Lunch break of the first Honda CRX Challenge Test Day. It was an excellent PR exercise for everyone. We raised over a thousand pounds to help Bob go to the Seoul Para Olympics.

Following on from Bob's great achievement I continued my first day's testing, which gave me an idea of the other Drivers, particularly those on the list. I can tell you here, and now it's going to be tough; I can't wait, my lap times are on par with Ackerley, a tad quicker than Tim Lee Davey.

# CHAPTER 41

## A LEARNING YEAR IN HONDA CRX.

I was so excited about racing in a completely different formula and one that would be very challenging.

All the motoring press were singing this championships praises, with editorials such as The racing press has hailed the new Honda Challenge as potentially one of the most exciting and competitive "one-make" championships to be introduced in the UK for many years. These Honda CRXs can be around 130 mph in their standard road-going form.

The 1988 CRX Championship will be contested over twelve rounds at all the British premier circuits, including Brands Hatch – Silverstone – Donnington – Snetterton- Oulton Park. The drivers will get a day of testing at the next race circuit on the list for all championship rounds. Exclusive testing other than for Touring Cars, Formula Three etc. is very unusual. I can only guess Honda UK did everything to attract top drivers, and it certainly was new to me and made me feel good. As well as that, racing for Team Edenbridge Honda came with loads of perks. Good quality hotels, including breakfast and evening meals.

I remember Team Edenbridge Honda arriving at the circuit for the first time, it was at Brands Hatch. I was gobsmacked. It was a beautifully presented articulated trailer that took the three Honda race cars with ease, and the trailer was kitted out with storage compartments on either side the whole length of the trailer. Once parked, the team got to work fitting an enormous awning the entire length of the side of the trailer. The three Honda CRX race cars looked stunning parked under the awning. (by the way, I'm still pinching myself) it's only been six years since I was a pupil at the Brands Hatch Racing School.

Team Edenbridge Honda was a three-car team competing against another thirty-five beautifully prepared Honda CRX. Race cars with highly motivated drivers.

We are at Brands Hatch for a couple of reasons; it was press day for the 1988 Honda CRX Challenge, and it was our first exclusive test for the first championship race. We felt as a Team, in particular, us drivers, we would fair well in the first round at Brands; we do know it well. The exclusive test went very well, with Andy Ackerley topping the times with 54,04 seconds. With Barrie Wizzo Williams second and myself third, Tim Lee Davey was further down the field. The Team were all happy, as was our Chief Peter Briggs. We need to turn a significant day of testing into great qualifying on the coming Sunday, followed by a good result in the race.

Race day soon arrived; there was plenty of interest in these cars from the press and public; I was approached by many that followed me in ff1600 and wanted to wish me luck which was excellent and encouraging.

Qualifying never produced the results we all anticipated, we ended up much further down the field than expected; Ackerley again pipped me on the time sheet, which is so annoying; at least I beat TLD. I do, however, need to outqualify extravert Andy Ackerley. Hopefully, in the next Qualifying at Snetterton!

The race was just as disappointing; we drove our nuts off but couldn't match the front-wheel drive experts in the other teams.

We went away disappointed, our mid-week testing had put the team and drivers on a bit of a high; but our lack of front wheel drive experience certainly showed, we went away knowing that we had much work to do. Both Andy and I felt the front wheel experts knew how to set these cars up, giving them a tremendous advantage, somehow the team and drivers need to try and find out what they are doing; in the meantime, we need to get testing and try to see if we can find something ourselves.

# CHAPTER 42

## THE WILLHIRE 24 HOUR RACE AT SNETTERTON CIRCUIT, NORFOLK

By chance! Tony Lanfranci asked if I fancied doing the 1988 Willhire 24-hour Race at Snetterton. I gave the offer a lot of thought, and decided that as this was a one off race, I could fit it in without affecting the Honda CRX championsip. The team would consist of Tony Lanfranci, Mike Jordan, and me (providing I can put up the £1000 required) Tony and Mike Jordan were big names back then.

I knew the boss Peter Waller from Cellnet very well; he always asked for me as his instructor; I was one of only three race drivers to get a free mobile. The other two are Damon Hill and Nigel Mansell. In good company there. Anyway, I thought, why not ask him? Cellnet can have good exposure on the car, plus I was racing for the Blind, which would be a good link. Peter was fine and sanctioned the sponsorship; he then announced they would sponsor Damon Hill in Formula 3 next year. Fantastic news. I got back to Tony to confirm that I would like to accept a drive in the Class A Sierra Cosworth.

I'm so excited; pinch myself again; I was a Brian Jones Motor Racing Stables Pupil just six years ago, and now I'm co-driving with top drivers Tony Lanfranci and Mike Jordan. This news has given me a boost to my lacklustre start to saloon car racing.

I let Peter Briggs know what I was doing, and he said, " OK, no worries, I will let you have a caravan with a 4x4 tow car for the weekend. All are free of charge. Thanks, Peter, you're a star.

I couldn't wait to let Tony know; we had a bolt hole to rest whilst waiting for our turn to drive.

The race wasn't for a couple of months which felt like ages away; actually, waiting went like a flash; a week to go, I was getting all the race information, our garage allocation was superb, and we were garage No1 which sounded like maybe TL has pulled a few strings.

We were next to Ian Taylor of the Ian Taylor Racing School. Luckily I raced on the circuit earlier in the year in the CRX.

We had to get there on Thursday for much-needed practice,

I called Peter Briggs to let him know when I required the 4x4 and Caravan. It will be ready for collection on Wednesday; I arranged to be there mid-day. I was ok with towing as we had a caravan several years earlier. I got to Peter's Edenbridge Honda Garage at midday. When I arrived, the 4x4 was connected to the caravan and was ready to go. Peter took me around to point out a few things and sent me on my way.

I'm nearer the Dartford Tunnel at Edenbridge, which is good. So off I go, Snetterton, here I come. I felt OK; no dramas. The 4x4 seems to tow well on these country A and B roads. As I joined the Motor Way, the whole thing felt wrong, and I don't know why; if I slowed down, it tank slapped. If I try to drive out of it, the same tank slaps, and it gets worst; I've only been on the Motorway for five minutes, and I'm shitting myself.

I decided to slow down and get onto the hard shoulder. Whilst taking this action, a high-sided lorry flashed by.

The caravan changed from tank-slapping to Rocking! This caused both sides of the caravan, firstly the left side tips over to touch the road, then back up, next, the right-hand side does the same, which happened in a flash. Next, the front of the 4x4 lifted off the ground, and with that, the whole thing, 4x4 and caravan, swapped ends, leaving the vehicle facing the oncoming traffic. There were horns etc., going off everywhere. I came to rest in the middle lane with lorries, cars etc., using the outside lane and hard shoulder to miss me.

It was like something out of one of those extreme crashes you see on the Cinema Screen, luckily, everything stopped; I had help from a few lorry and car drivers. We all managed to unhook the caravan from the 4x4, turn everything around, and park up on the hard shoulder. The side door of the caravan came off worst, and we used brute force to close it. However, before we did that, we could see what caused it to be so uncontrollable; the guys back at Edenbridge Honda had loaded it wrong, and all the weight was on the back of the caravan, making it light on the towbar. Everyone that day did a marvellous job. Thanks, guys.

That was one lucky moment, and to be honest, a miracle I was able to carry on my not-so-merry way to Snetterton. The rest of the journey was good; no dramas, thank Christ. I even got a wave from Tony Lanfranci as he overtook me; if only he had been 30 minutes earlier, that would have been another story.

Thankfully I arrived safe and sound at Snetterton Circuit. With plenty of time to park up and join Tony Lanfranci and Mike Jordan for a few beers in the Circuits Club House.

It's the first time I've raced in a 24-hour race, particularly with two great names, I'm still pinching myself. Looking forward to tomorrow when there will be a driver's briefing regarding the 24-hour race. Followed by free practice, plus in the evening, every driver has to complete a few laps of night time driving, which should be interesting.

Testing went well; our times were good, third quickest overall, and for me, more importantly, I was second fastest in our team, Mike Jordan quickest, me second and Tony Lanfranci a tenth behind me. I was thrilled with that.

Night-time driving was dark and slightly foggy. Mike Jordan was first, he did six laps, then came in, reporting no problems with the car. Next up, Lanfranci,who said he would finish his fag and then be with them. He smokes sixty to eighty a day. All good! Out goes Tony for his night laps; he does his six or so laps and then pits. I'm next and very nervous. I remember the Team vividly saying, whatever you do, touch nothing as you get into the car, and the same as you get out of the car.

Out Tony gets, in I get and remembering not to touch anything, I get myself comfortable allowing the Team to tighten my belts. Once done, I give the thumbs up and out I go.

The first thing I found was how dark it was and how bright the cars were coming up behind me; I felt it would be ok and not to worry, probably because I was not used to this driving. As I came over the start/finish line the team gave me an inboard, I thought that was strange; I'd only done one lap. I pitted, and to be honest; I was going to anyway, as I couldn't see fuck all. In I go, I'm at a standstill. I beckoned a team member across to say I couldn't see a thing, to which he replied, yes, TL turned the lights off. Apologies from the team lights on now; out, I go. "I could see" thank fuck for that. Nice one, Lanfranci. That was much better. I was the quickest in our team. Wait till I tell the other Instructors back at Brands.

Job done, big day tomorrow. Qualifying mid-morning and the Willhire 24-Hour Race starts around 4 pm. I need to get some kip. We qualified second overall, so the front-row slot for us. Tony Lanfanci to start the race, Mike Jordan second with me third. Initially, we will drive for 2 hours each, then decide to alter if necessary.

The time has come for pre-race photos, with our Cosworth Sierra sitting proudly on the front row and ready to go, I join Tony Lanfranci and Mike Jordan for photoshoots and editorials.

30-minute gong sounds—giving teams, spectators, sponsors etc., time to clear the grid. Then comes the 15-minute gong, followed by the 10 minutes—time for drivers to climb into their cars. The team hurry off to find our driver TL, who's having a last-minute fag. Tony, unhurried, wandered back to the Cosworth, which was waiting for him on the front row. With just 5 minutes until the start, Tony needed to get his helmet on and strapped in the car. Did he make it? Of course, he did, with 2 minutes to spare.

This race will be a pace car start; I think two laps behind the pace car, showing flashing lights on the roof. We will be looking for the pace car flashing lights to go off; this informs us that the pace car will peel off into the pit lane at the end of this lap. And the race will begin. All good; the 1988 Willhire 24-Hour race has started.

Tony is doing a great job holding station behind the leading car, the BMW of Ian Taylors Team in garage number 2. Two hours seem to go on forever; well, it's longer than a Grand Prix.

Next is Mike Jordan, another two-hour stint which is going like clockwork; Mike is a very smooth driver and looks after the car, the ideal driver for a 24-hour race. We are still in second place, with only twenty-hours to go. He ha ha. It's my turn next.

Mike's two hours are up, and he's due in the next lap. I've got my booster seat because I'm a short arse by name and a short arse by nature.

I'm watching Mike approaching. He pulls over to our garage; we help drag him out of the car; I then try to slide in as majestically as possible; Crew do my belts whilst others fuel the car. All seems to have gone smoothly. So out I go for my first stint in the Willhire twenty-four-hour race.

A twenty-four Hour race is all about driving smoothly and not tearing the arse out of the car, so a couple of seconds off the pace would suffice. My two hour stint flashed by. It was good in the daylight; my next drive time will be in the dark of the night. The following stints for us went well; that's a couple of outings for each of us. At the moment, we are looking in good shape to take maybe top honours (we shall see), I decided to get my head down in the wonky caravan whilst Lanfranci and Jordan took their third run; I wanted to be as fresh as I could for my morning two hours in the daylight. I couldn't wait.

I couldn't sleep much and heard Lanfranci's unmistakable voice. I checked the time and thought he should still be doing his third stint. Rolling off the bed in my race suit, born ready to race, I kick the caravan door open. Like a cowboy exiting the Saloon Bar, but not in anger, if you remember, it got buggered in the road incident on my way up to Snetterton, therefore a good kick was required to get it open. As I stepped down from the caravan, I was right. It was TL, smoking a fag, and not looking happy. I have learned if Lanfranci looks unhappy, tread gently and let him make the first move, a bit like coaching an injured lion to calm down. I gave it a minute or three, then gently asked TL if he was OK. He paused and took a big suck on his fag. Then he exhaled, and before all the smoke had left his mouth, he blurted out it was the fucking gearbox, the gear stick came off in my hand. (there's a joke there, but daren't say it) The team did their best to repair the damage, but sadly without success. The Willhire, 24-hour race was run for us.

We were all pissed off; race drivers always brushed the disappointment aside and began looking ahead to the next race. On the bright side of things, we could pack up and get away before the rush after the race ends.

I have to say I enjoyed the experience; it was very Carnival, with a fairground and food stalls everywhere; lights around Snetterton Circuit made it look and feel so different to a typical race weekend.

That's another tick in the box to say I've competed in the Snetterton Circuit Willhire 24-hour race.

What an extraordinary few days! And now back to Honda CRX!!

Patrick Watts; dominated the first year; he was at the sharp end of the field all year, apart from the odd off. Patrick's nearest competitor was front-wheel drive specialist Paul Taft; out of a race car, Paul was a lovely meek and mild Northern Lad; inside a car, he took no prisoners and fought for every inch of tarmac. Paul is a fantastic driver.

The next three or four races were similar to Brands and Snetterton. We could only make a disappointing midfield; trying as hard as we could, we couldn't find that last half a second.

Halfway through the year, Peter Briggs commissioned CRX front-runner Paul Taft to spend a day with us to advise us on how to drive these pocket rockets and set the car up. I shouldn't expect him to tell us everything; I certainly wouldn't.

We couldn't wait to see Paul Taft operate, or Tafty as he's known; Peter Briggs very quickly got Tafty along to Silverstone; initially, he's not how one expects a top-flight race driver to look; he wasn't exactly in his first flush of youth. What I did discover was that he was very organized. He explained everything in fine detail.

Tafty asked one of us to set a lap time in our car; he would then get in the car to see what he could do. Andy was quicker than me; therefore best he set a time. Andy set a time, and then it was Tafty's turn, which unexpectedly was a tad slower than Ackerley, which put a smile on the Extrovert's face. Tafty got out of the car and said four words, which we frequently heard over the next few months, and they were (It's not quite right). He drove the car into the booked garage for the test day and got the mechanics to alter a few things.

Once the adjustments had been made Tafty drove out onto the circuit, there was an improvement, but he still wasn't happy. (It's still not quite right) each time he went out, his lap time improved until he was happy.

Tafty was happy by mid-afternoon; it was our turn now, and both cars were available to set up. Out we went, I must admit to being somewhat under pressure; if you can't stand the heat, get out of the kitchen. We did several laps, and I managed to stay with Ackerley all the time and was quietly confident I was on par with his lap times; I was right and happy that our lap times were within a tenth of each other, and even more pleasing, not far from front-wheel drive ace Paul Taft. Tafty's day with us paid dividends; Ackerley and I benefitted most as Tim Lee Davey wasn't present on Tafty's day.

The rest of the year, we got better and better, but sadly not relatively quick enough to challenge the first four "front wheel experts". I managed to get the odd good result for the rest of the year; mine is a second at Castle Combe.

It wasn't very reassuring. I was used to winning; I was used to front-row qualifying. The sponsorship with Canterbury Mortgage Centre was for a year only; I didn't expect them to sponsor me for a second year, but thank them for supporting me in 1988; without them, I wouldn't have been able to race with Edenbridge Honda's superb Team. Need to find a Team and sponsor for 1989.

Peter Briggs, Boss of Edenbridge Honda, was desperate to get a winner on board. He offered Tafty a drive (a free drive). I don't blame Peter. He is a big name in the racing world and very used to winners, which Andy Ackerley, Tim Lee Davey or I couldn't do for him.

Tim Lee Davey decided not to contest another year. However, Andy and I weren't ready to throw the towel in. so we needed a sponsor and team. We went our separate ways.

# CHAPTER 43

## 1989 HONDA CRX WITH DENNIS BUNNING, ISLAND GARAGE, STAFFORD.

I found it challenging to raise funds to race CRX for another year. I read in Autosport magazine that Honda dealership owner Denis Bunning was looking for a driver to join him in his second CRX car, as his front-running driver Rob Hall was taking a sabbatical for a year.

Bunning's Honda dealership, Island Garage, sponsored his racing; it was his first year of racing, making him a courageous man to jump into the deep end of racing in this highly competitive championship. I called Dennis; we had a good chat, and he asked me to come up to Stafford for a chat, which sounded promising. I took my good friend and advisor, Ken Hall, with me, who is very switched on and it's good to have someone with you.

We managed to visit Dennis Bunning within a couple of days. His dealership was pretty impressive; this made me feel good about racing for him even before I looked at the cars. Ken and I went to Dennis's office; although I'd raced against him the year before, I didn't know him, probably because I was a bit further up the grid than he was.

Denis was a lovely man; he said he was in it for fun but would like someone to put one of his Island Garage Cars further up the grid. He was hoping his driver Rob Hall would stay another year, but Rob stepped down, hence the Autosport advert.

I saw an opportunity here, so it was time to sell myself without going over the top. We were with Dennis all afternoon, coming away with a drive for 1989. We finally saw the two Island Garage "Stafford" CRX Race Cars. They had their designated area, and both were sitting there looking great and ready to go. So time to shake on the deal and go home with Ken and I chuffed at the outcome.

Dennis never mentioned money, so we both felt it was a free drive as long as I could put my car further up the grid. Only time will tell. At least I'm in a race car for 1989.

Racing for Island Garage was different, laid back, with no urgency and certainly thrifty, for instance, new tyres were never heard of. I even raced the first race with last year's rubber; needless to say, the chances of getting the car well up the grid would be impossible. So what do I do? I had no option but to stick with it, hoping something would come along.

Dennis was a diamond and never asked for a penny; I enjoyed being with the team; there wasn't an ounce of pressure, so why complain? even went to Ireland and raced over there.

I'm not sure how, but I struck a deal to race Martins Down's Getem ff1600 at Mallory the same weekend that I was in Dennis's CRX.

Never done this before, and I can tell you, it was fantastic being with the Getem Team again, even if it was only for one race. The weekend was usual for the CRX qualifying midfield, but Martin Downs Getem went straight onto the front row alongside Mallory Park's top ff1600 driver, Mark Bryan.

Dennis Bunning was quick to remark how good I was in the single-seater and why couldn't I put his CRX on the front row. I thought, if I had new tyres and a good set-up, I would certainly have qualified much better. It was a great weekend, mainly doing a one-off race for the Getem Team, led by the one and only Martin Down.

I continued to race for Island Garage Stafford for the rest of the year, I didn't expect any good results and didn't get any. In a way, I was pleased the year was over. I'm not used to being an also-ran; let's hope 1990 will improve.

# CHAPTER 44

## 1990 HONDA CRX IAN TAYLOR-AB GLASS-VIC LEE.

This year was a mix-and-match year because search for sponsors was thin on the ground.

The first person to rescue me was Ian Taylor of the Ian Taylor Racing School, Thruxton. Ian was a great race driver in his own right, he's raced ff1600 very successfully, and I think F3. As well as saloon car racing, Ian competed in the 1988 and 1989 Honda CRX Challenge.

I got to know Ian through his BMW Drivers Days, and I worked as an instructor on them; those days were some of the best. It took a while to be accepted, but finally, I was. Ian employed many of the top drivers of that era. Mike Wilds, Andrew Gilbert Scott, Ian Flux, Bill Combes, Tiff Needell, to name but a few.

Ian Taylor heard that I was looking for a drive this coming year.

Ian contacted me and explained that due to business commitments, he would be unable to race in the 1990 CRX Championship. I was looking for sponsorship to compete in this series again and as I was someone that had already contested the championship, he would like to offer the drive to me, complete with sponsorship from Wagon Finance which would pay in full for the remaining six races. Would I want to take it on? Let me think! A nanosecond later, I said yes.

Ian went on to say that Vic Lee Motorsport, of Touring Car fame, will run the car; Vic ran Will Hoy and Tim Harvey in the BTCC both one the title with Vic Lee Motorsport.

Ian instructed me to call Vic Lee and make an appointment to see him to get the ball rolling, which I duly did. Within a few days, I was at V.L.M Headquarters, which was very impressive. My eyes were almost popping out; there were six mechanics/engineers smartly dressed in VLM corporate clothing, and the whole place was spotless. Vic's office was up on the mezzanine floor, well-positioned so he could look over his magnificent empire. I knocked on Vic's door, he asked me to get myself a cup of tea and he would see me quite soon. Quite soon turned out to be a good hour later but I wasn't going to complain for a second, considering I'd landed a free six-race drive.

Vic had a chat with me, albeit a reasonably swift one. I was introduced to the guys that ran the Wagon Finance CRX; now, I feel comfortable as I am getting to know my team. As always, the guys in most race teams are a fabulous bunch. I was on my way home by 7.30 pm feeling chuffed that Ian Taylor gave me his CRX drive. What a great guy.

It was only late February. The first CRX race isn't until April, but I have a day's testing at Silverstone in March; I can't wait. I was looking forward to seeing how I would fair in the ex-Ian Taylor's CRX, and I was expecting a more competitive car than Dennis Bunnings.

As I turned off the main road into the entrance of Silverstone Circuit, I noticed a race car transporter slowing down to wait for the barrier to lift. As I drew nearer, I could read who it was: My new team Vic Lee Motorsport. I felt excited, and whenever I entered a race circuit, I got nervous; even now I'm retired, I still get the same feeling, although not to the same degree as when racing.

I followed the Vic Lee Motorsport Transporter to the back of the pit lane garages. Then parked up and allowed them to reverse onto our allocated garage. For whatever reason, I was more nervous than ever; I couldn't put my finger on why; it may have been I had big shoes to fit, taking over from Ian Taylor.     Strange, I've won so many races but still get nervous, and sometimes I doubt my ability, which I know is daft. I noticed the team was rolling the Wagon Finance Car into the garage; I decided to give the team time to get organised before getting involved. Thankfully I had already met the team back at Vic Lee Motorsport's unit; I did my usual and went straight over to each, and everyone shook hands, and after a little chat individually, I now relaxed and wanted to get testing.

It's still early, another hour before testing begins; my car is already apart from bleeding the brakes, which shouldn't take long.

Team Boss Vic Lee is on his way; I thought he only got involved with the Touring Cars; it was great to see him showing interest; more pressure but good pressure. I've worked with Vic several times on the Club 89 Driving days, which Rosemary Palmer ran. They were super days; once the driver had joined the club, they would come along and get instruction from top race drivers, such as Barry Wizzo Williams, Tiff Needell, Mike Wilds, Tim Harvey, Vic Lee, Will Hoy, David Leslie, Chris Hodgetts and good old me.

Then at the end of the day, we would give them a few hot laps in the Club 89 BMWs.

Now, where was I? Sorry, I've gone off on a tangent, oh yes, waiting for Vic Lee to arrive, as he has the brake pads for the car. Vic arrived in good time to fit them before general testing began. The team instructed me to get my overalls on as the car was ready. Off I shot for a quick pee, and back to check I'm comfortable in the car. Just one or two adjustments are required then out I go, I was beckoned out of the garage by the team, then directed by the guy swinging his arm to continue up the pit lane. Off I drive up the pit lane stopping at the red light, then waiting for the pit lane Marshall to give me the signal to go.

How good was this? It seemed to take forever to get back into a race car, the car felt good, and more importantly, it was good.

It was a cold early March day; the tyres required a few laps to get them up to a decent temperature. After a few laps, I could feel the car was responding well to faster entry speed; I was starting to feel good in the Wagon Finance car.

I was given the inboard after I had completed half a dozen or so laps, for a chat and tyre temperature check. I made my way up the pit lane and parked outside the team garage. I stayed in the car, the team took over, pushing and steering the car backwards into the garage. I'm out. The team are checking the tyres to see if they have reached the optimum temperatures. How I've missed all this attention.

My lap times; were excellent; I was half a second up on the other CRXs out there. I was delighted but had to understand those comparable lap times were not against the likes of Patrick Watts or Paul Taft, and the fast-improving Andy Ackerley. We had fabulous days testing; I was the quickest all day. By the end of the day, another five CRXs had turned up, making my lap times even more impressive. Sadly the klaxon sounded the end of testing for the day, I went home happy and looking forward to better results this coming season.

The six races in the Wagon Finance car moved me up the ladder as a driver, and I managed top-ten finishes in all six races thanks to Vic Lees's help in driving style.

I built a good rapport with the Wagon Finance hospitality guests that attended every race, I did my best to keep Wagon Finance interested in using motor racing as a platform to entertain their clients and use it as part of their advertising campaigns. Unfortunately, Wagon finance was only going to use motor racing for three years and this was their third year. It was regrettable for me; at least I had six races handed to me by Ian Taylor, for which I was eternally grateful.

In the meantime, knowing that I needed to find another drive once the Wagon Finance sponsorship ended, I tried high and low to secure support, but without luck.

# CHAPTER 45

## CLUB 89

I remember, by chance, whilst I was racing at Mallory Park with the Dennis Bunnings Island Garage team, last year, Rosemary Palmer, the owner of Club 89, was a spectator

During the interval, Rosemary came into the Paddock to say Hi; she said that she had heard over the tannoy the commentator say that I had taken him around Snetterton in the CRX and how exhilarating he found it. He also said that I was looking for sponsorship to enable me to keep racing. Rosemary suggested we meet up for a chat.

I got in touch with Rosemary, explaining my predicament and why I was without a CRX race-prepared car. Could she help? I was aware that Banks Honda of Bury St Edmunds had a driver that raced in the Honda CRX Challenge but stopped racing and returned the car. Maybe she could use her charm and persuasive ways to let her driver (Me!!) race for Banks Honda in 1990.).

Rosemary was not one to let the grass grow under her feet; she called me in a couple of days to confirm she had a deal with Banks Honda, and the car was ready to collect.

# CHAPTER 46

## WHIPPET MOTORSPORT

I haven't got a team to run the Banks Honda at this particular time. I started searching and remembered Honda CRX Driver Steve Waudby, a rapid driver run by a chap that lived way up North, Les of Whippet Motorsport, a great Northern Lad that knows his way around a race car.

Steve Waudby had moved on to another championship; I called Les to see if he would be prepared to run me in the remainder of the 1990 Honda CRX Challenge. We talked for hours; he sounded passionate about racing and would like to accept the challenge by running me. Great result.

I soon discovered that my teammate would be the very quick, highly-rated James Kay. He's going to keep me on my toes, I bet.

Although the Banks car was in Race spec, it needed quite a lot of attention to bring it into competitiveness. We had to miss the next race as there was no way Les could get the car ready in time; I had to think I was lucky I was racing. Les proved to be a red-hot engineer, exuberating me with confidence; this is the first time I have felt like this since ff1600 with Rob Cresswell Racing Services. I have longed for this moment to return, and now it has. The time I had with Les was terrific. He was a down-to-earth, straight, talking Northerner; he gave me a car that was good enough to win; sadly, I wasn't, but I now think I will; only time will tell. My best result with Whippet Motorsport was second; my worst memory with Whippet Motorsport was at the Birmingham Super Prix Street Circuit.

I've never raced in a street race. The Birmingham street race is, without a doubt, the most enjoyable, most exciting race I have ever entered, it was so tight, so bumpy; I loved almost clipping the Armco that, in places, was level with your shoulder; you had to be inch-perfect to get a quick time.

In practice on Friday, James and I were in the top four, with Ackerley being the fastest. Les was excited; getting his two drivers in the top three had made his day. He couldn't stop cuddling James and me, silly sod. Qualifying was take place tomorrow, Saturday.

Qualifying - Les and his helper got us out first for the session; it was paramount to have some space; being amongst so many cars on this circuit would make it so difficult to get a quick lap. The Klaxon sounds for the start of qualifying; I follow teammate James out onto the circuit. We are first and second; we must make the most of it. James is in front, going reasonably quick whilst weaving to get heat into his tyres; I'm doing the same; if he's doing it, then it must be the way to go. We continue at a pace giving us a clear lap or two before we get mixed up with other drivers; on the third lap, I see James is on Pole; I'm second; I have to keep it up; on lap four, Ackerley takes over Pole I'm second James third. And that's how Qualifying ends with Ackerley on pole, me second, James Kaye third; what a result.

Extravert Ackerley had put himself under pressure because he approached the Birmingham Branch of Halfords with a very clever deal. His proposal was for Halfords to give his Son a top-of-the-range racing Bike. Halfords would be given prime advertising exposure on Andy's CRX. If Andy won the Birmingham Round of the Honda CRX Challenge, Halfords would give his son a Bike of his choice, if he lost, Halfords would have received all that exposure for free. Nice one, Andy.

After qualifying, Les checked the cars over. James and I agreed that the setup was spot on, apart from a spanner check. As a Team, we are in a good place. Hopefully, Les's Whippet Motorsport may end up as giant killers later this afternoon. Wouldn't that be great?

And now for the race. Expectations were high. James and I were relaxed and not showing any signs of nerves, which is very unusual for me. Our time to race seemed to come in a trice which is what a driver likes; there's nothing worse than twiddling your thumbs waiting for hours; this was ideal. Before no time, we were sitting in our pocket rockets, waiting for the Marshall to signal us out onto the grid. I had my starting plan in my head, as I always do.

We are all stationary in two rows; I'm in the front of one row, and Ackerley is in the front of the other row; I can see him gesturing to me, which I ignore. The light goes green. The Marshall waves us on, so off we go. As I drive out, there is a healthy number of spectators. What an atmosphere all very new to me, these street circuits, but a fantastic feeling.

We are positioned on the grid by the excellent grid Marshalls; I am sitting on the front row, next to Andy, with nothing in front of us. It's been bloody ages since I've been this far up; it was some four years ago when I was dominating ff1600.

First, I follow extravert Pole Man Ackerley the entire warm-up lap until we get back on the grid. I was all fired up and ready for the lights to turn green.

The lights turn green. Ackerley makes a great start; thankfully I tuck in behind him. I am managing to keep my teammate James behind me. As we turn into the first corner, Bristol Street Motors Corner, a ninety-degree left brings you immediately to British Telecom International Chicane, a left-right-left section because the Armco is level with your shoulders. The speed through this section feels tremendous, exhilarating and bloody quick, whilst placing the car inches from the Armco.

The sensation of speed on this Birmingham Street Circuit is mind-blowing; there's barely anywhere to relax. No, there's nowhere to relax or take your eye off the ball, apart from Peter Barwell hill. As you leave the chicane and approach the massive roundabout, which, as mentioned earlier, is so bumpy, you can feel your bollocks being sat on as your CRX takes off several times. I'm not sure if you need a perfect line through this section, just big balls, which I don't have anymore, thanks to this bumpy roundabout. I will have to delve into my overalls later to see if they are still there.

Once the roundabout is over, you head slightly downhill passed the Fish Market on your right. The pits and paddock are situated there. No time to stop for Cod and Chips, as the slowest corner on this Circuit is looming up; Redex Corner, which is a very tight left-hander. No room to overtake here, just a follow-through corner. But I am trying to get a quicker exit than Ackerley in the hope that he will make a mistake and I can thread my way through. After this very tight section, it's slightly uphill to an awkward lefthand Tandem Turn, which will bring you onto the start-finish line. Andy pulled away a tad, my fault; I was doing my damndest to keep my teammate James behind me, which I did for several laps. All was going swimmingly. James was as good as being in my boot; he was that close I knew he could only get through if I made a mistake, which I was managing not to do; we continued to race like this for a few laps, finding that I was quicker in some areas but he was faster in others.

James seems to catch me up along Belgrave Middleway, the approach to the Fish Market and the very tight left-hander Redex Corner. I managed to pull away a yard or two as we climbed up towards the awkward left-hander, Tandem Turn. I'm not sure what happened as I began to negotiate Tandem Turn, but the car felt good. I started my left turn, suddenly, the car kept going left; I was a passenger; I hit the Armco on the left heavily, followed by my car bouncing back into the centre of the circuit, taking out my teammate too. Bloody hell, I have some explaining to do when I get back to the pits

Oh, what could have been? I don't have to explain the feeling back in the pits. Gone were the smiling cheery faces; I could have crawled away and hidden, but no, I've been there before. But I never took out my teammate; all sorts of things were going through my mind, mainly the cost of the damage.

And would I be responsible for James Kays's damage? As always, once the situation calms down, things slowly get back to normal; James covered the cost of the damage to his car, and his atitude was "That's motor racing fella"

So we are all a happy team again, which was fabulous; I did, however, have to miss the next race, but the one after that was Silverstone National which I love. I netted a third at Silverstone, Mr Ackerley on the top spot again; I'm not too disappointed as I seem to be at the sharp end most of the time now.

Sadly, Les White, the Whippet boss, decides to pack up. It was a crying shame. I seemed to have been left high and dry, with a few races still to be run in the 1990 season.

Again by chance, another team, A & B Glass from Sudbury, got wind of my situation; Teams Boss Ray Byford got wind of my dilemma and came to my rescue, offering to run me for the rest of the season. That's certainly taken the pressure off, and guess what? I will be on the same team as Andy Ackerley, and I look forward to the challenge.

A & B Glass are a very professional team no cutback at all in this team; although I didn't seem to excel with A & B Glass, my few end-of-season races were most enjoyable.

As we got nearer and nearer the then of 1990, my thoughts were very much on the 1991 Honda CRX Challenge.

I have been trying to raise funds for next year but finding it difficult with my new job as Snetterton Manager taking up a lot of my time.

Sometimes I wonder how I manage to find sponsors, it's all about not giving up, having a lot of luck, and by chance, it happens.

I got sponsorship from Colvin, a Printing Company based at Caterham, a professional Race Company. And CVA is an Engineering Company. Luckily I am now sorted for 1991, talk about by the skin of my teeth.

Looking forward to 1991, I just got to find a team or talk to the team I'm hoping to tempt into the world of a front-wheel drive one make saloon car championship.

# CHAPTER 47

## MORE OPPORTUNITIES WORK-WISE

Meanwhile, I'm lucky enough to be offered several opportunities work-wise, as was my old enemy but now best buddy Chris Albert Hall.

Once you become a known name in this industry by doing a good job and being a front-running race driver, you are halfway to getting asked to work elsewhere. Back then, they also wanted instructors with personalities. Albi and I met the requirements. We were well established at the Brands Hatch Racing School, both now Senior Instructors, continuing to train more and more instructors; we were a bit of a double act. Similar to when we raced against each other, which was different.

Andy Ackerley had stopped being an Instructor, moving on to new horizons. Andy began working for manufacturers on their track days. Several car manufacturers loved the idea of promoting their new models on famous race circuits where selected guests could try the latest models and have the opportunity to drive around a race circuit, and on most occasions, be taken around the circuit at speed by the race drivers/instructors.

Ford was into these days in a big way in the late 80s. "Drive and Survive" ran the days, but farmed the actual circuit side of the operation out to Andy Ackerley, which was brilliant. Andy knew us from the Brands Hatch Racing School; he approached us to work for him on these days, which covered almost every race Circuit in the United Kingdom. To fit all this additional work into our already busy schedule is going to be interesting.

I'm already working at Millbrook Proving Ground for my Brands Hatch Racing Boss, Tony Lanfranci and taking guests around the inner circuit in a Ford Escort Cosworth, which is ideal for giving the guest the experience of what it's like being driven at speed; it's one hell of a ride. Hard work, but what a way to earn good money; I had the pleasure of working alongside great drivers such as Tony Trimmer, Le Man winner Dickie Atwood, World Rally Driver Roger Clark and good mate Mark Blackwell. These were fabulous times.

John Stevens ran Audi Sport Hi Performance days exclusively for new owners of an Audi Sport Saloon Car, which was part of the package for anyone who purchased an Audi Sport. Included in the package was a stay at a five-star Hotel, generally in grounds well away from the hustle and bustle of significant roads etc. We would join the Audi Sport owners for the evening meal every night they stayed. Typically the instruction lasted for three days, and by the end of the last day, the aim was to get the Audi owners to an excellent standard of fast circuit driving. These days were complex and tiring but rewarding; by the end of the last day, we were all knackered. But no one ever complained as the daily rate was terrific. The downside was that we had to drive home at the end of the last day, straight after the day was over. When you think we went as far away as Knockhill, Scotland, it's one hell of a journey! Again no moans; we got a fuel card plus 28 pence a mile and this was back in the 80's!

As well as Audi, I was involved with several other major manufacturers and I had the opportunity to travel to many European countries including France, Spain, Belgium, Holland and Italy. I was also fortunate to be involved in with film shoots, one in particular, Nissan Terrano, taking me all over Spain, including fabulous Seville, and being taken up in a balloon. Again hard work and long days but a great experience.

It's now 1990, Just ten years since I arrived at Brian Jones's Motor Racing Stables as a Pupil; I still have to pinch myself regarding my journey.

They say "Don't look back" but I can't help it, how lucky was I to have become a race driver at the best time ever? Very lucky indeed.

Motorsport has just started to evolve in the last ten beautiful years. I've seen Motorsport progress in leaps and bounds, not always for the best, but that's always the case with everything that needs to move forward.

# CHAPTER 48

## JOHN WEBB SELLS BRANDS HATCH LEISURE

Brands Hatch Circuits Ltd. consisted of Brand Hatch, Snetterton, Oulton Park and Cadwell Park circuits and was owned by John Webb. John had decided to sell the company to John Foulston and this would mean change, something that will always happen when a company changes hands. The day to day running of the company was taken care of by John Foulston's daughter Nicola, who certainly wasn't a shrunken violet. I got on quite well with her, and she often asked me to give race tuition to her family or essential personnel.

I was beginning to feel the workload getting to me. If I was not instructing at Brands, I was driving up the motorway to some distant hotel to stay for a few days or even sometimes a few weeks, working for a Car or Corporate Company. I felt I was ready for a change.

Boss Tony Lanfranci sent another pupil to me for an initial trial; I always try to check whether I will have an easy ride or not; I'm sure it's true with most instructors; you can tell before they get in the car.

The guy looked a bit nervous on this occasion, and I was happy with that. I removed my sunglasses (rude if you don't), shook hands, and introduced myself. He's a tall, handsome bugger; he says "Hi, my name is Lance Ellington". I asked Lance to get in the driver's seat and make himself comfortable; I always assisted with the seat belts, as not many pupils would have experienced using them before. Once Lance was all belted up and comfortable, I made my way to the passenger seat. I asked Lance if he had done anything like this before, and he told me that he was looking to go racing if he came up to the plate.

I then asked him what he did for a living, and he told me that he was a singer and his late Dad was Ray Ellington, an English Singer drummer and Band Leader, best know for his appearance on the Goon Show. Wow!

To cut a long story short, Lance went through school and drove exceptionally well; hundreds out there now know Lance through Motor Racing and being the lead singer in BBC's Strictly Come Dancing.

Lance finished being a pupil at the racing school and I lost track of him until one day the phone rang, I answered, and immediately I recognised his unmistakable voice. He said, "Hi, Rick; this is Lance Ellington. I've asked Brian Jones for some advice as I would like to try saloon car racing and could he point me in the right direction". Lance went on to say "Brian said have a word with Rick, he may be able to talk to the team that he drives for". I was flattered that Brian Jones had suggested that I might be able to help and I told Lance that I would see what could be done. More of this later.

For personal reasons, Les White of Whippet Motorsport has decided to pack up. Which is a great shame; I enjoyed being one of his drivers. Whippet Motorsport has undoubtedly been the team to turn me into a front-runner, for which I was forever grateful.

# CHAPTER 49

## BY CHANCE

I received a telephone call from Brands Hatch Business Development Manager Richard Green, asking me to come to his office as he has something to discuss with me. By chance, I happened to be instructing at Brands that day, so I arranged to go and see him during my lunch break. Richard Green has done well getting to such a high position in the new Brands Hatch Leisure Ltd.

I didn't know what Richard wanted to discuss; I knew Richard; he was good to talk to, so it wasn't one of those situations when you think, what the hell does he want? So off I pop lunchtime, tap on his office door and enter. Richard was very welcoming, a good talker, and a bit of a laugh, how I like it to be.

Before long, he opened the Autosport at the Classified section and said "Have you seen this", to which I replied, "No I haven't". It read something like this, Brands Hatch Leisure Ltd is looking for a Manager of Snetterton Circuit. Richard said he felt I would be a good candidate for the job. If I would like to apply for the position, he would forward my name with a recommendation to Nicola Foulston.

I told Richard I would certainly consider it, but I needed to discuss it with my wife Anne; it's going to be one hell of a decision. Richard agreed, saying he would await my decision but not to leave it too long, as they would like the existing Manager of Snetterton, David Ross, to take over the management of Oulton Park as soon as possible. Plus, they are receiving applications from others.

We had a tremendous informal chat that lasted more than my lunch break; I got Richard to call Lanfranci to explain I was going to be late, he was fine. We shook hands. I left with my head full of questions about the for and against becoming Snetterton Circuit Manager. It was difficult carrying out the instructor's work that afternoon, my mind wasn't on instructing and because I felt it could cause a safety problem I went to the Control Tower and asked Lanfranci if I could take over the timing as I wasn't feeling too well. (you little liar) Tony was fine about it.

My thoughts: what's Anne going to think? After a few hours, I got home and mulled over becoming a Circuit Manager. I have to admit to feeling somewhat excited about it. As I said earlier, I was looking for a change within the Motorsport Industry, which this job certainly was if I was to be offered it. After lots of to-ing and fro-ing with reasons for and against applying for this position, we both felt it was a chance to be able to do something different. So there we have it! I'm going to apply for the job of Manager of Snetterton Circuit.

I quickly called Richard Green, asking him to send me an application form for the job. He was delighted to hear the news. The application form arrived the next day; it was pretty straightforward. I duly filled out the form and dropped it into Richards's office the next day. A few days later, I received a phone call from Nicola Foulston inviting me to attend an interview for the job. At first thought, it was all moving too quickly— nothing I could do about it now apart from change my mind, which I wouldn't do. The interview was in a couple of days; do I wear my suit or go casual? I chose my suit.

So here we are on interview day. Nicola Foulston's was in the old building to the right of the Kentagon. In I went to reception and was told to take a seat, Nicola will see you shortly. It wasn't long before Nicola appeared from her office, shook my hand invited me into her office.

Slightly sarcastically said mmm, brown shoes, Mr shortle, I thought she approved, but soon found out she didn't.

It was very informal, whilst chatting; Nicola would ask questions about why I wanted the job, what I could bring to the table to help the circuit improve turnover and appearance etc. The interview I felt went well; I think because I decided to go without any expectations, I came across as not being someone desperate for the job. However, after the interview, I was hoping I would get the job, but I will have to wait; Nicola has a few more applicants for the position.

I haven't got the job yet, but I walked out of Nicola's office buzzing, feeling good about myself. It's the opportunity I was looking for, to do something different but stay within the Motorsports Industry. I will have to wait for the letter to see if I landed the job. I tried to play down the fact that I could soon become the Manager of Snetterton, but to be honest, I wanted that position; waiting for the acceptance or sorry Rick, you were unsuccessful this time, seemed an age.

About a week later, the letter arrived; it was a posh envelope with an inscription from the office of the Chief Executive.

So here I am. I had the letter but was frightened to open it and worried I hadn't got the job. It was an age before I plucked up the courage to open it; finally, a deep breath, here I go; I slide a knife along the top of the envelope, not wanting to damage it. It's open ready to pull out. I pull it out slowly, similar to when I used to receive my bank statement, expecting bad news. The letter is now out of the envelope; I very slowly begin to unfold the letter. It begins Dear Rick etc. etc. etc. I get to the significant bit, and it said, Congratulations, we have decided to offer you the position of Snetterton Circuit Manager, wishing you every success. I was ecstatic, jumping up and down, effing and blinding. I've got the job, the effing job, and I never thought for a moment I would.

Nicola Foulston would like me to take the job over within the next month; I have so much to consider, our home back at Selindge in Kent, Anne's position at the local Tesco super Store, could she get a transfer; the answer was yes, in Thetford just a few miles down the road. I would get a Company Car with a fuel Card; we would live on-site in a spacious rent-free Colt bungalow next to the circuit office. Ideal for work.

During the period I was the Manager, several well-known race drivers knocked on the Bungalow door. One, in particular, Jackie Stewart, asked me if he could use my lounge as a meeting place for his two drivers racing in his F3 Team the following year; I called Brands to get the ok which wasn't a problem. Jackie required the use of the telephone, which he used nonstop for hours; he had one driver with him, the other was I believe, in Brazil and the discussions continued for hours. It started at 6 pm and finished around 11.30 pm., a long session. Jackie thanked Anne and me for the use of the bungalow lounge and presented us with a box of Heineken non-alcoholic beers (his F3 Team Sponsors). He said his goodbyes and left.

We were glad to get our bungalow back; even if it was Jackie Stewart it was good to see them go. I don't think his drivers did that well. I think this was the start of Jackie's climb to owning an F1 Team before it was bought outright by Ford and was renamed Jaguar Racing, with drivers Rubens Barrichello, Johnny Herbert, Jan Magnussen and Jos Verstappen. I did remind Jackie that I had worked alongside him at the Brands Hatch Racing School carrying out the briefings, where he would front Corporate events for Ford.

I won't go into great detail about being the Manager of Snetterton Circuit; apart from the fact that I enjoyed my time there, the staff were terrific, and it was the best job I've ever had. Whilst I was busy getting into this fantastic job, I was trying to focus on the 1991 Honda CRX Challenge with the new team and hopefully, Lance Ellington.

# CHAPTER 50

## THE 1991 HONDA CRX CHALLENGE WITH GETEM GD RACING

I spoke to Martin Down, yes, the very same, the man who put me on the map back in the early 1980s turning me into a winning driver in his unique ff1600 Getem GD race car. I have enticed him to run me in the Honda CRX Challenge, with Lance Ellington as my teammate. Martin was more than up for the challenge, as was his general go-for; just a thought, Ken Baker, along with Martin's two young sons Nathan and Jason. Nathan now lives in America and continues to keep the Getem chassis alive by building and racing it with great success. Jason gives his late Dad's final creation a few outings each year at Brands, not missing the Martin Downs Trophy Race in November.

Martin is highly focused and will put 100% into race car preparation. Consequently, I began spending lots of time with Martin. Oh, how I missed this; it was like the old days. I did wonder if working on Saloon cars would be as rewarding for Martin as his beloved Getem ff1600 (A couple of of-inches off-the-ground race car). I certainly hope it is.

It was time to get back to Lance Ellington to tell him the good news. He will be joining me in the 1991 Honda CRX Challenge. Martin and I met Lance at a Hotel near Brands to discuss the coming race season. When we arrived, I introduced to Lance one of the most important things we do, the Team Hug. As yet, Lance hasn't got a CRX race car; there aren't many available; only those drivers deciding to give it up would have cars available.

So, the first job would be to find a car; Lance searched all the race mags, as did Martin, but only two were available. Martin wanted to go and view the vehicles with Lance to ensure the condition etc. Great news, Lance has a race car; Martin helped choose the deal; if I remember, the seller even delivered it to Martin. So we are a two-car Honda CRX Challenge Team and I look forward to working alongside the man who spotted something in me back in 1982.

Working with Martin Down is unique; it's different from any other team or teams I have been involved with since I began. Looking back, Martin is so amazing, apart from the fact he's become a legend, respected as a genius in Formula Ford 1600. The Getem GD Racing team consisted of Martin Down, his trusty helper Ken just a thought Baker, his two boys, mere whipper snappers at the time, Jason and Nathan, his behind-the-scenes wife Judy, and occasional helper John Haggerty.

I was so excited and as usual couldn't wait. Martin and I would run through things over the phone most evenings, it was even more interesting having a second driver in the team, singer and son of Ray Ellington – Lance Ellington.

Martin put his eyes over both cars, getting them ready for pre-season testing, which would be at Brands Hatch. Lance wanted to do well; I enjoyed coaching him. He would listen and take on board everything; I applaud him for jumping into the deep end; the Honda CRX Challenge was a top one-make saloon car championship.

Lance's driving soon improved in leaps and bounds; his lap times would already put him around fourteenth out of the twenty-eight drivers contesting the CRX Championship. Martin and I were very impressed with him. He's settled in remarkably well, is always smiling, and is a great asset and teammate.

The first race approaches. I'm looking forward to seeing how I fair in a CRX prepared by Getem GD Racing. Martin is a deep thinker, constantly chewing things over, and always talks to me before making radical changes. I'm used to working alongside Martin; I remember some radical changes we tried in testing; nine times out of ten, we ended up where we started. I have to accept; these are early days for Getem running a saloon car. However, I'm quicker than previously, not much but quicker.

Being the Manager of Snetterton seems to be good for me. Although the job is pretty full-on, I have a good team behind me that allows me to feel confident they would cope whilst I'm away, particularly under manager Maria Skitmoor. She was amazing.

I do seem to feel more relaxed when racing; it could be a few things, maybe the job, I love it, or perhaps being back with Getem GD Racing; I love that too. The first two races proved bloody difficult for Lance Ellington; Martin and I felt he was doing better than he gave himself credit. Because he improved each time out, he always brought the car back relatively unscathed. I'm thrilled with the progress; in the top five in both races. I have a good feeling about this year, plus it's great having a teammate like Lance. I couldn't have wished for better.

Martin is getting into the CRX, and we are now trying different settings etc. I know we are there or thereabouts; I need more from me and Martin to find that little bit of magic he has up his sleeve. It's fantastic to be back where I started; it's like coming home.

Over the next few races, the improvements kept coming. Lance is already creeping into the top ten; he drives an immaculate race and never puts a foot wrong; I feel its time for him to start putting his elbows out; I had a quiet word; I could almost hear his brain taking in my comments along with the concerns in his eyes. Do you know what? Next race, he went out and did it. Bravo, Lance; another barrier you've gone through. Meanwhile, I've picked up a couple of third places and a win at Cadwell Park (I love that circuit). We're getting there, Martin.

All is good in the Getem camp; Martin is now buzzing quietly.

Donnington is a circuit I love and I remembering my first time with the Getem ff1600; I put our car on the front row next to Perry McCarthy and Johnny Robinson.

It is a scorching summer's day, and Honda have exclusively hired the circuit for our Honda CRX 1991 Championship. It's getting to that time when magazines start tipping drivers that could win championships; I'm now in the running against Andy Ackerley and Russell Grady. So yes, the good old Getem GD Racing Team are in the pot.

We felt we had found something that may give us the edge, the CRX was performing well with a full day of testing against all the CRX teams present, we would find out if that was correct. Martin was never one to rush. We had all day; even I agreed five to six good laps is much better than thirty average laps because that is all you would expect in this hot weather. The tyres will overheat after six hot laps. I have always liked to do five to six hot laps, then pit; as I've said previously, I would get pole on my second to third lap, so why change what works?

So that's the plan for testing, five laps, then in Martin to work a bit of magic each time, then out again; I love testing. It's rewarding to find more in the car and more in you.

We carried out this plan all day; by eleven o'clock, I was quickest by half a second, and by mid-afternoon, I was still fastest and was also under Patrick Watts's lap record. It's one of those days you can live over and over again. We were all so relaxed. The day was perfect; I did my bit, came in, and sat on the tiered steps in the pit lane looking right above the Getem Boys working away; when things are going so well, it makes you feel good inside.

Lance was doing well. I don't have to worry about him much these days; if he needs help, he comes and talks to me. I am so pleased with how Lance has progressed. Give him a year or two. I'm sure he will make the podium.

Today was the best day I've had whilst in CRX. Martin Ken and Nathan were there; young Nathan takes it all in and remembers those days, as I do with pride. Best day ever, and with the team that gave me the opportunity. It's nearing the end of the day; our work done, nobody in the pit lane can live with us, not even extravert, and as good a driver as he is, Andy Ackerley.

Ok, time to pack up, Lads, and go for some supper.

It's now qualifying and the race! The weather is still warm and sunny; our neighbours Colin (Cole Boy) and Annie are there supporting me. They are a lovely couple; Colin enjoys motor racing and his hobby is photography which he's damn good at; Colin kindly offered me sponsorship, not with cash, but by driving Anne and me to the races in their big Mercedes, FOC. This type of sponsorship helps expenses more than you think; motor racing is the length and breadth of the UK. When you add it all up, it's quite an expense.

The other benefit I get is fantastic photos. Thanks, Cole Boy.

Brother David is there, giving me support in his no-nonsense way. I think deep down, he's pretty proud of me. He hides very well, although I get feedback from Brother Peter on the odd occasion, with remarks like David said Rick is a bloody good race driver. I'll take that, and that's good enough for me.

I feel very relaxed with an inner belief like my ff1600 days, which is excellent; I can walk around the paddock with a spring. Knowing unless something goes dramatically wrong in qualifying ie, the car has a problem, or I mess it up, I should be on a Pole; I hadn't felt like that for a while.

Whilst whipper snapper Nathan cleans the car and Ken just a thought Baker, makes perfect cups of builders tea. Martin is checking the CRX over, ensuring it's as perfect as this genius can get it; if your race car is performing well then the driver will perform well too. If he doesn't, you can blame the car; it was lapping under the lap record in testing yesterday; no pressure Rick.

We must be the first CRX out for qualifying; that's Ken, just a thought Baker's job. A clear track helps me to have any chance of matching those impressive times I did in testing. Well done, Ken. Excellent job; we will be out first; let's do this. Like yesterday's testing, qualifying went like a dream; I was the quickest the whole session, putting the Teams Getems CRX on the pole by almost half a second, which is a significant advantage. Alongside me on the front row was fast-improving Bill Gibson, with Russell Grady third and a somewhat disappointed Ackerley in fourth. It may not be very reassuring for Ackerley, but not for me; I was hoping he would make a slow start and get held up whilst I get away.

Just waiting for the timesheet to be available; Martin never makes a mistake, so I'm confident enough to know I'm on the pole. I can't wait for the race; needless to say; the team are buzzing; young Nathan has a smile from ear to ear, and teammate Lance Ellington the same; you would think he was on the pole, and Martin and Ken were delighted are now keen to get Team Getem's CRX's ready for the race. What a fabulous little team we are.

I am looking forward to the race at 3 pm.

It's time for a nervous pee before we go to the collection area.

The usual stuff is going through my head; Martin is nearby in the collection area in case there's a problem. The excellent Marshalls are watching us all, waiting to signal us to make our way onto the grid; sitting in the collection area seems to take forever. Thankful not too bad today.

Whilst sitting on the grid waiting for the green flag to send us on our warm-up lap, I look in the mirror at my rival, Ackerley, seated on the second row. The Start Finish Marshall lifts the one-minute board, followed by a waved green flag to signal we can proceed with the warm-up lap.

I try my start, which seems reasonable, then continue on the lap weaving to get heat in the slick tyres; it's a warm day, so there is no need to overdo the weaving; I can remember as if it was yesterday, my mind was one hundred percent focused on my start.

Ok, Folks, this is brilliant to be on Pole; I look at the apex to the first corner of Redgate and do what I used to do when on the Pole in ff1600; that's a shout that corner is mine.       I'm on pole; I'm feeling confident, not looking anywhere other than straight ahead to the Apex of Redgate. Here we go. Count down boards shown; Lights show red, got my revs up to what I feel is right; I'm in first gear, they go to green.

I make a flyer, already half a car's length in front of Bill Gibson, before we've left the grid, totally focused on the Apex, not bothered by what's going on behind me; I'm at the Apex and able to take the perfect line for the exit. I can't settle just yet. I check my mirrors to see if I can see Andy Ackeley; I notice he's up to third getting the jump on Grady, thankful; Bill Gibson has kept Andy back; my job now is to make a break, get away from extravert Mr Ackerley as much as I can, I know full well he will try to hunt me down.

I know that genius Martin Down has given me a fast car; if I drive as I know I can, I should be able to keep him at bay. By lap six, I had pulled out a commanding lead; Andy had managed to get past Bill Gibbson; I told myself to relax, don't overdrive, and keep smooth; the Donnington circuit requires a smooth driving style.

I feel in control and measure my distance using markers on the track. I enjoy watching Andy behind me, mainly down the Craner Curves into and out of the Old Hairpin. His car often seems sideways; I'm not sideways at all. Martin has certainly given me a fantastic car to drive.

We have four laps to go; it seems in the bag; we all know it's not over until the chequered flag; I have a good cushion from Andy; I do begin to relax a tad, making sure I still have a good gap, I am playing with him a bit, the sort of thing he would do to me. We finished the race with Andy catching me a little, but I controlled the whole race.

I could see the sheer excitement with my amazing Getem Team; they were jumping up and down behind the Pit wall. It has been a magic few days, and Andy and I broke Patrick Watts's lap record five times.

I do my lap of honour waving to the crowd and notice my lovely wife Anne at Regate with Cole Boy and Annie, and I am waving away. Boy, I feel great; then it's back to the pit lane for the presentation of Trophies and interviews. Andy was terrific, and he said "I couldn't catch Rick; he was too quick for me today".

Martin was beaming from ear to ear; Lance Ellington was there to congratulate me. Sadly his race wasn't so good; that's motor racing, as we all say. Lance didn't receive any damage, so both cars were unscathed.

I would undoubtedly put these last few days amongst the best of all the races I have won. The Getem Team, Martin Down, I know I keep saying this, but he is a genius.

Martins's fabulous Team gave me three wins, a lap record and second place in the 1991 Honda CRX Challenge, for which I thank him and his team.

Unfortunately, I decided to stop racing for many reasons, mainly because I was tired of chasing sponsorship. Although I did the odd race over the next few years, mainly for fun, I knew the time had come to hang up my helmet.

At first, it wasn't easy to choose where or how to finish my book BY CHANCE, but it wasn't long before I knew exactly how to finish this book; It had to be the Honda CRX Challenge with Getem GD Racing at Donnington.

# CHAPTER 51

# MARTIN DOWN R.I.P 15TH NOVEMBER 2019

After reading my book thus far, you've got to know my feelings for this remarkable man.

Sadly Martin passed away whilst working on his beloved Getem in his workshop. His son Jason called to inform me of his Dads passing, which was so upsetting. The Funeral was attended by so many from the racing fraternity, including Linton Stutely, Neil Tofts, and Chris Maliepaard, and it was beautiful, which was followed by a celebration of his life, precisely what Martin would have wanted.

Ironically I was coaching a Lad that wanted to race ff1600.

Just a few weeks before Martin passed, I visited Martin to see if he would be interested in running this lad in the Champion of Brands. Martin said yes, so we got the ball rolling to the stage when we were ready to proceed.

Martin, to me, was an extraordinary person; he didn't require airs and graces to be unique; he was special. An individual that I trusted implicitly; he gave me a chance to win many races. I will never forget our first win; it was so exceptional for both of us. We both knew from that moment we had a car and, hopefully, a driver that would send Getem and me on our way to a chequered career, which we did.

I loved being with Martin or talking to him on the phone; our conversations seemed to only last five minutes; in fact, it was usually at least an hour.

I cherish the time I was fortunate enough to race for his Team. GETEM GD RACING.

Martin may have left us, but he will always be around; he became a legend in Formula Ford, and many teams and drivers that got to know Martin miss him so much too.

This fantastic individual was quickly becoming known for his knowledge and unique ideas.

Many teams would talk to him for advice on testing and race days.

Martin proved he wasn't just great with ff1600; the year he ran me in Honda CRX, I achieved three wins, one lap record and finished second in the Championship.

Thank you, Martin.

Love Rick and Anne xx

Lance Ellington - a singer with records to his credit is now in his first year of racing. He is competing in the Honda CRX Challenge Seen here with team mate and race winner Rick Shortle.
Both cars are run by Getem racing

# CHAPTER 52

## THE FOLLOWING YEARS

For the next twelve years or so, I continued to earn my living within Motorsport.

I worked for the following companies.

Geoff Mason Fusion Events. Geoff's corporate days run at Millbrook Proving Ground were far beyond their years; I worked alongside many great race drivers, such as Tony Lanfranci, Tony Trimmer, Barry Wizzo Williams, and Derek Bell. We took the guests for a couple of fast laps around a small twisty circuit that was exhilarating for the guests and great fun for us.

Other activities included flying Helicopters and Karting which I owned and ran and an ABS exercise, which everyone enjoyed.

The guests drove exotic cars around the famous Millbrook Bowl and the whole day was a great, fun run; super slick day.

Geoff, thank you so much for your sponsorship, which allowed me to make a comeback to racing. Your phone call that afternoon telling me I've succeeded in getting sponsorship from Fusion. will always be a memorable one.

Drive and Survive. Paul Catlin and Andy Neal. I had the pleasure of working for Paul and Andy for several years; the only drawback was being away for two to three weeks. Luckily, I had an opportunity to open a small karting business. This opportunity came by chance from Drive and Survive. Whilst working for them on one of their corporate days, as we were talking, Andy mentioned that Drive and Survive had a few karts that they used to include in their events; they stopped using karts because they kept getting damaged and caused them embarrassment most of the time. I asked if I could have a peek at the karts, and Andy was happy for me to have a look. I looked around; the karts seemed a little tired but still usable; they just required a bit of care and attention.

I could feel my brain working overtime; I thought I could do something with these, but at the moment, I'm not sure what.

I had a chat with Andy and asked him not to sell them just yet, as I have an idea that we could both benefit; he said no problem, spikey (my hair all gelled up back then)

I came home excited, thinking, how can I make a few karts work? I don't have a track. I did know that Drive and Survive moved to Crowthorne, a proving ground similar to Millbrook but on a smaller scale.

I decided to put a proposal together and present it to Andy Neal and Paul Catlin. I knew of their events and that Crowthorne had space to put down a kart circuit. My proposal suggested that D&S approach Crowthorne to rent a piece of ground to allow them to make a kart track for corporate events.

If D&S liked the idea and got thumbs up from Crowthorne, I would run karting events, with D&S getting priority for their events. D&S loved the idea; I just had to wait and hear Crowthorne's response.

Within a week, Crowthorne responded positively; it was a resounding "Yes". The deal was that we only paid when we used it; it was dirt cheap too.

Thanks to D&S, I have a small karting business. Something I've never done before; for a while, it was difficult, but thankfully it came together, and work began rolling in; with D&S now including karting in their driving days, we soon had regular bookings from them.

We were getting swamped, making things a little complicated; I had help from a couple of people, but I had to be present at every event to ensure they ran smoothly. My only solution was to find someone who could come in as Manager, to run this side of the business, freeing me up to carry on with the other lucrative work I have done for quite a while.

I already had someone in mind; it was a guy named Noel Wilson; Noel ran his own business, supplying Marshalls to companies that require Marshalls for their Corporate Events. One of the companies was Fusion Events, where I got to know Noel.

I offered Noel the position of Track Manager for RS Karting, which he accepted. Once Noel came on board, the little RS Karting business increased; it allowed me to be office-bound, taking the bookings and organising things. Which worked extremely well

I trusted Noel, so I gave him carte blanche at the track, which proved to be the right decision. Our kart track ran like clockwork. Noel continued to work for me for several years; he did a fantastic job for RS Karting and often told me I was his best boss. Likewise, Noel, you were an outstanding Employee.

We were fortunate enough to have several celebrities at the RS Karting events, these included: Tom Cruise (Lap record holder!), Les Ferdinand, King Husain of Jordan, several England Football players, Alistair Stewart, and Tiff Needell to name but a few.

Vauxhall was another Motor Company to do things in style. Tony Lanfranci ran a small select team of drivers which I was lucky enough to have been included, along with Tony Trimmer, Hugh Marshall and Mark Blackwell.

These were fabulous days, we all got a brand new Vauxhall top-of-the-range car, which we collected from the Vauxhall headquarters at Luton, and we kept for the six to eight-week tour; it also included a fuel card. I would have thought this Vauxhall tour was the biggest of the lot; we were the envy of all the other instructors who worked in different areas.

Not racing allowed me to work on these events and earn decent money. I was extremely fortunate as most of these events continued for six years or more until the Motor Companies began to feel that launching their new models on race circuits was becoming too expensive.

Noel Wilson's "MS" and a "Bloody Silly Idea".

I would like to say a few more words about Noel Wilson

Noel began to suffer from severe back and leg problems confining him to bed quite often for several days.

Noel called me for a chat, but this time with sad news; he explained he had been for tests and been diagnosed with Multiple Sclerosis. Since being diagnosed with MS in 2013, Noel's condition has worsend and sadly, today, 2022, Noel uses a wheelchair.

At the very point of being diagnosed with MS., Noel came up with what he described as a "Bloody Silly Idea".

The "Bloody Silly Idea" was called "THE CHALLENGE." Noel would set an official lap time for an eight mph mobility scooter for every circuit/venue in the UK for his charity venture, collecting money for his charity. Noel named his fundraising idea "Motor Sport For MS." Noel hasn't stopped there, he is always thinking up all sorts of "Bloody Silly Ideas".

His initial target was £20k; however, 2022 contributions have rocketed to over £51k.

Sadly Noel now finds things a little bit more difficult, does this deter him? Not on your nelly.

Noel has fantastic supporters and helpers for which I thank every one of you; there are too many to mention individually, but I'm sure you wouldn't mind me thanking the Yukie Toones. for everything they do to support "Motor Sport For MS".

Noel and his lovely Wife, Karen, along with his regular team of helpers, need to be thanked and congratulated. Here's to raising even more for MS.

To donate,
Log into Noel's website www.motorsprortforms.co.uk

Thank you.

# CHAPTER 53

## THE PETER ROGERS CELEBRATION PARTY

On August 6th 2022, Lucy Rogers and Ian Flux organised a party in the Kentagon at Brands Hatch to celebrate the life of her beloved Brother Fast Peter Rogers or "FPR" for short.

They invited anyone that knew Peter, all drivers that raced against him, all teams/mechanics, engine builders etc. it was a wonderful evening seeing people one hasn't seen for years. To name a few
Lucy Rogers. Ian Flux. Roger Pedrick. Howard Drake, builder of the Laser ff1600 that FPR successfully raced, Graham Fuller of Minister Engines, Perry the Stig Mc Carthy, John Robinson, Pete Townsend Tony Trimmer, Bob Lambert and my hero Rick Morris.

Ps Fluxie was on his best behaviour.

The Peter Roger Memorial Trophy Race was kicked off with a superb evening's entertainment, a great way to start the fully packed race day that Lucy Rogers, Ian and I will experience the next day.

On race day, an entire grid of twenty-eight ff1600 raced in this fabulous event. Seeing them on the grid, ready to battle to win the FPR Memorial Race, was genuinely remarkable and moving.

Prize money was given to the first, second and third in all three classes, with Cups being presented by Lucy Rogers and myself on the start-finish of the Brands Hatch Grid. It provided a superb backdrop of the Hospitality

Suites and the rise of the track that disappears as the notorious Paddock hill bend dips away from sight.

The overall winner Jordan Dempsey took home £1250 with Colin Queen second and Lucas Romanek third. Matt Rivett, the FPR driver in a 1991 car, finished a respectable fifth and former Champion of Brands Chris Goodwin, an instructor at the same time as me, finished in ninth place.

The race was superb, certainly fitting to commemorate The great. "FPR" Fast Peter Rogers.

Thanks to everyone for making it such a memorable, emotionally exciting day.

Team FRP would like to thank Ben Edwards and Scott Stringfellow, and Val Adaway for their behind-the-scenes help and advice, also, Gary Hawkings, for the superb photos. You all helped make the weekend a fantastic event.

# CHAPTER 54

## THE ORANGE ARMY

And now something about the Marshalls, better known as The Orange Army

My book would not be complete without thanking the best in the world for everything they do, rain or shine. Of course, it's the Orange Army

Over the years, I cannot remember how many times they pulled me out of the tyres, loaded my race car on the breakdown truck, and then my ride of shame back to our spot in the pits.

On several occasions, the Orange Army worked alongside the duty doctor who checked me over whilst they extruded me from my ff1600, as well as other race cars during my time as a race driver. Noteworthy was a particularly nasty off going into Paddock Hill Bend Brands Hatch. My Van Dieman swapped ends as I turned into this high-speed downhill corner; from that moment on, I was a mere passenger in the car. I made my way strapped in the cockpit, helpless whilst the rear of my vehicle led the way toward the tyre wall on the infield, thinking this was going to hurt, I was right, it bloody well did. Hitting it, travelling backwards with tremendous force, I received four cracked ribs and whiplash.

I raced before the Hans Device was available; for those who haven't heard of a Hans Device, it was invented several years ago to protect race drivers from serious injury to their necks. The Hans Device now has to be worn by everyone who races and since its introduction, this device has prevented many drivers from serious injury.

I was lucky to get away with it so lightly. St. Johns Ambulance took me to St Mary's Hospital Sidcup. The Marshalls and Doctor did a fabulous job; nobody panicked, and they were super cool.

A few years ago, The Marshalls invited me to spend a day waving flags, using the radio, and trying to understand what Marshalls do to prevent us from getting hurt. It was one hundred per cent concentration, and I soon realised there was more to Marshalling than I previously thought. Following the exercise to let a race driver experience what it was like to be a Marshall, I've had nothing but praise for them from that day forward. Like most Race drivers, I didn't give our Marshalls a second thought. We must! Because without them, there wouldn't be motor racing.

Marshalls are a wonderful group of individuals that love doing their job. It's non-paying; if you approach them about the subject, they respond "We do it for the love of the sport, plus we have the best seat in the house!".

In the nineteen eighties, I raced several times against Peter Rogers in ff1600; Peter was exceptional. I enjoyed some close racing against him; he was hard but fair, a Lion in a race car, but a perfect gentleman whilst out of the race car. As I mentioned earlier, destined for the very top, Peter Rogers was the real deal.

A secret donor approached me to explain he knew Peter Rogers and was very sad that Peter lost his life at Donnington in 1987. The secret donor wanted to thank the Orange Army and all those who helped in trying to save Peter.

As well as donating £1000 to the Orange Army, the donor organised the ff1600 race at Brands Hatch called the Peter Rogers Memorial Trophy Race, to be run in August to remember the loss of Fast Peter Rogers.

We involved a great guy named James Beckett, who everyone knows; James is Mr Organiser of Formula Ford Events. He has a say in the Formula Ford Festival's different ff1600 championships across the UK and the Walter Hayes at Silverstone.

Without James Beckett, it's fair to say Formula Ford would be far less if James weren't steering the Ship. Thank you, James, for helping us put the Peter Rogers Memorial Trophy Race together.

The months leading up to the Fast Peter Rogers event in August 2022 were busy and very enjoyable. The secret donator, who I have never met, was generous to a fault and was a man of many ideas, which he would ask me to think about and get back to him.

The secret donator contacted me while selling my first book Full Circle An Autobiography. He initially purchased a copy and, within a week, contacted me to say how he enjoyed the book and that he runs a small club for friends. He would like to purchase another twelve books to give to them. Fantastic—what a sale.

It didn't ended there; he then decided to commission me by purchasing one hundred and fifty more of my books to give to the BMMC Marshalls on the day of the Peter Rogers Memorial Trophy.

We agreed to put the book, individually signed by my good self, the FPR Badge, and an insert about FPR in a presentation box. Even if I say so myself, it looked pretty good. I felt so good handing this gift out to the Marshalls at Brands before the meeting.

Thanking the BMMC. After the Marshall's briefing, all one hundred and fifty Marshalls were gathered around in a well-chosen area to show a good background for the photo. I gave a "Thank you for everything" speech", which got a round of applause. I followed by presenting a cheque for £1000 to the BMMC Marshalls

The Post Two Marshalls Trophy. Back in 1985, I was chosen by the BMMC Marshalls to receive the highly prestigious award, which was given out every year to the driver they considered to have been excellent throughout. I received my presentation at the end-of-year Marshalls Dinner at Brand Hatch and was invited to sit at the Top Table alongside John Webb.

It's great to join the list of excellent drivers with their names engraved on this huge Trophy; my name joins the greats - David Purley, Gerry Marshall. Karl Jones, and Mike Wilds, to name a few.

My book would not be complete without thanking the best in the World; For everything they do, rain or shine.

Of course, it's the Orange Army

# CHAPTER 55

------♦------

# R.I.P BRIAN JONES "THE VOICE OF BRANDS"

I was fortunate enough to visit Brian on the podium many times when presented with a first, second, or third trophy. I've known Brian for years, having worked for him on his events or the School Corporate days that Brian fronted.

Brian would always have time to stop and chat. He was an exceptional person.

Sadly Brian died of Covid, on New Year's Day 2021. He was 85.

Thank you, Brian, for everything.

Jackie and Isobel Epstein

Thank you both for all the help you gave me in my early days as an instructor and for all those enjoyable times working for you. You were simply the best and undoubtedly changed my life for the better.

------♦------

# CHAPTER 56

## 2022 STILL INVOLVED

After all these years, and finally, I've got the racing bug out of my system, I'm finding myself highly fortunate to be involved in helping up-and-coming drivers improve.

I'm now getting my much-needed adrenaline rush from seeing the drivers I have helped improve with help from me.

The drivers I assist just now give me just that, a couple of brilliant drivers. Ben Powney and Matt Luff. More later about these drivers.

By chance I found Alec Galloway, who was my boss, when I was a Plasterer's Labourer some forty-odd years ago, and as soon as he knew what I was up to, he immediately sponsored me until I retired from Racing.

When I retired from racing I approached Russell Houchin, a friend and sponsor for over thirty-five years, I asked him if he would like the idea of sponsoring a couple of race-winning drivers I mentor? to which he said yes.

I'm still involved with motorsport, but now the safer side of the tyre wall, and loving it. I wouldn't get back in a race car for all the tea in china, and it frightens me shitless just watching.

Back to Ben Powney and Matt Luff.

First, Ben Powney from Hythe, the link here is that in the eighties, we lived next door to his Grandad Cole Boy. In Sellindge Nr Ashford Kent. Once a year, in our garden, we would have a party to thank the race team,Cole Boy and his Wife Annie would roll up their sleeves and help organise the event.

The race car sat on the front drive, observed as they walked past to get to the Party.

Young Ben was about five at the time. Many years later, I found out he was racing, so I got in touch with him to say hello, and whilst chatting, he told me it was my fault he was a race driver; I asked why? He replied that he would dream about becoming a race driver because I let him sit in the race car.

It was a no-brainer. I introduced Russell to Ben, and both driver and sponsor hit it off immediately. Russell loves the involvement with Team Stella; the whole package couldn't have been better. Ben is a front-runner in Caterham, winning many races; I enjoy being there and giving advice if and when he requires it. Good luck in the future, Ben. Here's looking for a Championship Win in 2023

21-year old-Matt Luff.

In 2020 A friend of mine called me to ask if I could help and advise his Nephew on moving forward with his vision to becoming a top race driver. He continued to explain that Matt was a World Kart Champion in his mid-teens but didn't want to go down the single-seater route.

Having had a few races myself in 2018 with "AREA MOTORSPORT" in the Milltek Honda Civic Cup Championship, I saw the championship was tough. Not many slouch drivers are contesting it, so an excellent place to begin, And Area Motorsport would be my choice. All parties agreed, including Matts's Parents and Matt himself and were happy to proceed.

I contacted Rob Baker, Boss of Area, to explain that I felt Matt was a young, sensible Buck with his head screwed firmly on the right way round; I would expect him to be a front runner from day one. On his first test day at Brands, Matt went under the lap record for the Honda Civic Cup cars by four-tenths of a second, which was a lot in anyone's books.

Matt is currently studying for a Master's in Entrepreneurship & Innovation after getting a 2.1 in his BSc (Hons) at the Royal Holloway University of London. Matt secured the 2022 Milltek Honda Civic Cup Championship title in a dramatic season finale at Norfolk's Snetterton circuit in October 2022

Matt admitted it was a 'dream come true to be crowned champion in such a thrilling climax, having finished runner-up in 2021. I am delighted, as is Russell Houchin, to have been part of his journey in what can only be as impressive—The first year, 2021; second overall in the Championship; the second year, 2022, Winner of the Championship.

Now that Matt has won the Championship, we need to sort out his next move, and no matter which way you go, it will be expensive. Ideally, we would like to move to TCR Touring or similar.

# CHAPTER 57

## WINDING DOWN

I have to admit I've enjoyed writing my second book, "By Chance", even more than Full Circle. It's given me such a buzz.

Every photo- news cutting etc., reminded me of a situation; be it a race situation or just chatting in the Paddock, it all rushed back.

Anne and I would like to thank everyone that have become friends over the last 40 or so years; all of you are lovely, funny, silly and yes, dare I say it, at times, highly professional. You know who you are, so there is no need to embarrass you, thank you for being our friends.

For me, it's been a roller coaster ride from the first day I started my journey on a grass bike until I decided to retire from racing.

A new beginning. Happily, it hasn't stopped there, as the Carpenters say, " It's only just begun". As you know, I'm already looking after a couple of drivers, which I'm enjoying immensely, so I will, at my pace, attempt to help them.

Who knows? Maybe another book in the future? Watch this space.

Thank you everyone.

# WITH SPECIAL THANKS TO

My lovely Wife Anne (with an "E") and my two girls, Tina and Julia, for putting up with it all. I now realise what a selfish sport motor racing is. If you wish to do well, one has to be focused, putting to one side other just as important essential day-to-day activities. Sorry about that!, Thank you. xx

Brother David, I'm sorry you lost your battle, and a shame you were taken whilst I was still racing. Thanks Bro. for your input. (you were priceless) and not forgetting my other brothers, Christopher and Peter for their invaluable help over the years. xx

Derek Gurr for mentioning Grass Track Racing.

Sponsor and Owners of AB Stores Brian and Celia Elmer.

Reading Racers for signing me up as one of their Riders.

Reggie Luckhurst's Help and advice.

Hackney Hospital, for putting me back together.

Brian Jones's Motor Racing Stables. Thank you for the superb tuition from top race drivers, and your closed School Races, which were an excellent way to have a taster, and planting the seed to try motor racing.

Martin Down GETEM GD RACING. For seeing potential in and offering me a drive in his unique Getem ff1600, and having the invaluable opportunity to work alongside Martin in his garage, making bits etc., for the car we raced at weekends. I gave Martin his first win in our second year of racing together, whilst contesting the Dunlop Autosport Star of Tomorrow Championship. Along with many wins in Martins's Cars contesting the John Player Special Champion of Brands Series.

Sponsor Brian Varney of Legal Services

Thank you so much, Brian, for taking me on this journey as far as you could. without a shadow of a doubt, without you, possibly none of this would have happened. Also, Thank you Brian, for introducing Rod Stephenson to me.

Johnny Weir Ashford Accident Repair Centre.

Auriga Engine Builders.

Sam Nelson, thanks for Damon Hill's ff1600 engine and the use of your ff2000 engines.

Dave Minister and Graham Fuller, Minister Engine Builders. Thanks for great engines and good publicity through the local press.

Steve Brown and Barry Osborne for use of your Sebron Hospitality Suite at Brands Hatch

Strand Glass Fibre

Cosy Burn

New Church House Restaurant.

Kent Consortium

Sealink

Rob Cresswell Racing Services. Thank you Rob, and Pipe smoking Dave Linstead for preparing the fabulous Reynard 84 to perfection, allowing me to bring so many wins for the Team. It was an absolute pleasure to race with your Team. Furthermore, thank you for preparing a Reynard 84 ff2000, allowing me to finish third overall in the BBC Grandstand Series on my first attempt.

Thanks to John Webb for his sponsorship when getting funds to race got tough.

Mike Fulmar Taylor Sports 2000.Thank you, it was a pleasure and an experience to race with your Team; sadly, I finished third, I couldn't catch you or Fluxie.

EdenbridgeTeam Honda Many thanks for asking me to join you in the 1988 Honda CRX Challenge. Your Team was highly professional; it was fabulous to spend a year with you.

Canterbury Mortgage Centre, Colvin CVA.and Atlas Car Hire. Thank you for your support in the Honda CRX Challenge in1988, 1989, 1990, 1991

Teams - Edenbridge Honda, Island Honda Stafford, A&B Glass, Whippet Racing, Vic Lee Motor Sport and GETEM GD RACING. Thank you, for without you, I would not have been able to have raced for four consecutive years competing in the Honda CRX Challenge.

Martin Down's Wife, Judy. Thank you for putting up with me coming to your home for several years every evening, Monday to Friday, to help Martin work on the Getem ff1600 inn the garage at the bottom of the garden. Thank you for the Earl Grey Tea, which I wasn't keen on, so I made out I liked it mixed with builders tea, which you kindly did for me.

It was lovely catching up at the Martin Down Trophy race in November 2022 at Brands Hatch Anne and I had a great day chatting with some of Getem's drivers and your two exceptional sons, Jason and Nathan. During our chat, Nathan jokingly remarked that I was at their house so often they thought that I was a long-lost elder Brother

Judy, as mentioned at Martins Trophy Race. See you in Spring 2023 for lunch.

Love          Rick and Anne

———◇◈◇———